J.P. MORGAN

SUMMER

READING LIST 2022

J.P.Morgan

BEING
PRESENT

EING

ESENT

tion at Work (and at Home)

our Social Presence

TURNER

Georgetown

Library of Congress Cataloging-in-Publication Data

Names: Turner, Jeanine, author.
Title: Being present : commanding attention at work (and at home) by managing your social presence / Jeanine W. Turner.
Description: Washington, DC : Georgetown University Press, 2022. | Includes bibliographical references and index.
Identifiers: LCCN 2021005290 (print) | LCCN 2021005291 (ebook) | ISBN 9781647121549 (hardcover) | ISBN 9781647121556 (ebook)
Subjects: LCSH: Communication—Technological innovations—Social aspects. | Interpersonal communication—Technological innovations—Social aspects. | Telecommunication—Social aspects.
Classification: LCC HM1166 .T875 2022 (print) | LCC HM1166 (ebook) | DDC 302.2—dc23
LC record available at https://lccn.loc.gov/2021005290
LC ebook record available at https://lccn.loc.gov/2021005291

∞ This paper meets the requirements of ANSI/NISO Z39.48-1992 (Permanence of Paper).

23 22   9 8 7 6 5 4 3 2 First printing

Printed in the United States of America
Cover design by Amanda Hudson, Faceout Studio
Interior design by Paul Hotvedt

Contents

Preface

For the last thirty years, I have been fascinated by what it means to be socially present. My first job out of college was as a salesperson for General Mills, where much of my focus each day was on trying to engage the attention of grocery store managers to sell more products like Cheerios and Gold Medal Flour. These managers seldom have time to talk with salespeople, so I would chase them around their stores, trying to get them to consider, adopt, and sell more of my products. While selling for General Mills, I also began teaching Dale Carnegie courses, where I helped people learn to present themselves and influence others, again focused on how to keep the audience's attention. I first started thinking about the impact of communication technology on social presence and attention after I returned to school to pursue my master's degree in communication at the University of Dayton. There, I started to learn about media choice and explored theories to explain how organizations and individuals make decisions about the type of technology to use based on the needs of their message in order to engage their audience. Here, I received my first email account and started thinking about the impact of asynchronous technologies on the way we communicate. It was at the University of Dayton where I was first introduced to the term "social presence"—or the perception of being present with another person.

UNDERSTANDING SOCIAL PRESENCE

In 1993 I moved to Columbus, Ohio, where I continued my graduate studies at the Ohio State University and where I watched as the internet developed into the World Wide Web. I started studying distance education and telemedicine. I was part of a research team that connected

Ohioans with hemophilia to a bulletin board system (this was before web browsers) using donated computers. I drove around the state, installing computers and modems and teaching people how to connect to the internet and meet other people with hemophilia. Many of the individuals I had the pleasure of meeting had never met a person with hemophilia before. This research took place during the early 1990s, when many people with hemophilia were also infected with HIV and, as a result, faced intense discrimination because of the ignorance associated with the disease. The ability to connect in a social support network, called the HIGHnet (Hemophiliacs in Good Health Network), gave them the opportunity to be socially present with others who faced similar challenges. It encouraged many of them to travel to Columbus for the first time ever and meet face-to-face.

My PhD dissertation explored the implementation of telemedicine within Ohio's prison system, and I continued to explore how communication technology both enhanced and detracted from the way we are socially present. I still remember meetings where our telemedicine team at Ohio State's medical center connected to the telemedicine system at Lucasville Penitentiary so the nurses from the prison could attend. It was my first experience with a hybrid meeting, a challenge that became incredibly common during the pandemic of 2020 and beyond but reinforced the strong need to develop an environment where everyone feels included and present. In one meeting, some of the participants at the prison site were dozing off since most of us who were physically present were involved in a complex discussion and we were forgetting to bring the participants on the videoconferencing site into the conversation. (Twenty years after this meeting, schools and organizations everywhere would be navigating this balance.)

EXPLORING AND UNDERSTANDING
MULTICOMMUNICATION

After graduating from Ohio State with my PhD, in 1996 the business school at Georgetown University (later named the McDonough School of

Business) hired me to teach courses to MBAs and executives about strategies for engaging their audiences through presentations, conversation, and writing. My research continued to explore telemedicine, and I also began examining the use of instant messaging. I had the opportunity to research the use of instant messaging at AOL. This was when I really started to become interested in how people could engage in multiple conversations at the same time. About one month after the terrorist attacks of September 11, 2001, I was conducting interviews and one person told me a story about how he realized he never really talked to his coworkers face-to-face, even though he had been working next to them in his cubicle for a number of years. He said he was very focused on his work one day when the power went out. At the time, AOL's headquarters was located in Dulles, Virginia, not far from Dulles Airport. Everyone stood up from their cubicle and looked toward Dulles Airport to see if there was some kind of problem because there had been much discussion about how one of the planes that was part of the September 11 attacks had flown out of Dulles. He told me that once everyone realized that the power outage probably had to do with nearby construction, they stood up and silently walked to the elevators. No one really talked with each other. He said people weren't used to talking with each other face-to-face. They would send instant messages to each other rather than walk to another cubicle. Wow! Stories like this drew me further into exploring social presence and what it meant.

Based on this instant messaging research, my colleagues and I developed the construct of multicommunicating to describe how people engage in multiple conversations at once. With the birth of the iPhone in 2007 and the rapid diffusion of mobile devices, this practice exploded. Now individuals were thinking not just about what communication channel to use to be socially present but also about how many conversations they could be in on one channel and still be socially present.

At about this time, my appointment at Georgetown moved over to the Graduate School in the Communication, Culture, and Technology (CCT) Program, where I was able to continue to study the impact of communication technologies on organizations and individuals.

CREATING A FRAMEWORK FOR MANAGING
SOCIAL PRESENCE

As I researched multicommunicating and its impact on social presence, I continued to learn from my students in the CCT Program and the business school. I had conversations with executives who had returned to Georgetown to pursue degrees, as well as executives who came to Georgetown for training programs. Many of the stories and interviews I have had with them appear in this book. I listened as executives, faculty members, students, and family members talked about how mobile devices were infiltrating their work and home lives. Over the past twenty years, I have talked with thousands of people, exploring their thoughts about social presence. My colleague Sonja Foss and I created a framework for managing social presence that draws from these ideas, and we supported it with academic research. This framework is the basis for the strategies that I explore in this book.

In the back of my mind, throughout my research, I wanted to write a book that could give people strategies and ideas about how to be socially present. I tried out ideas with executives and graduate students in my classes. I noticed that as more and more people were overwhelmed by the "always on" environment of mobile devices, I saw a surge in mindfulness approaches and ideas about how to be mindfully present—but not socially present. Along the way, I started a family and needed to continuously think about how I was navigating my own social presence between work and home with my husband John and our three children, Michael, Kate, and Andrew. I was actually finishing my book in the spring of 2020, and the idea of what social presence meant finally became salient to many as we learned what it meant to be socially distant.

When the world had to go into lockdown because of the COVID-19 pandemic, we all had to figure out how to use communication technologies to connect with each other so we could maintain work, school, and family relationships. Our work became entangled with our home life as we struggled to manage our social presence. And as the shutdowns persisted over the next year, not only did we learn how to connect in different ways but we also began to get used to what different types of being socially present meant. As I write this preface, in January 2021, we are starting to see the potential to return to more physical presence, in-person meetings with others, and reconnecting with friends and family members. This change will bring with it a host of decisions for both organizations and individuals. Before the pandemic, you might have thought of in-person physical presence as a type of "gold standard" or the "best" form of presence. However, the last year has shown you many options and helped you to see the benefits and challenges of in-person communication. The elimination of the stress and logistics associated with a commute or meeting travel, the ability to work during a meeting when no one can see you, and the opportunity to manage home and work from the same location has meant that when you can be safely in-person from a health perspective, you might still choose to be socially present in another way. What relationships, contexts, or meetings will earn in-person social presence?

WHY I WROTE THIS BOOK

I wrote this book to help you explore the complexities of social presence and to help you be intentional and strategic about the decisions you make on how and when to be socially present. In the next eight chapters, I describe social presence and the four choices you have available when making decisions about social presence. Each chapter concludes with reflection questions and exercises to help you further explore these decisions in your own relationships. I have always had a hard time separating the challenges that mobile devices bring to both home and work environments, and the pandemic illustrated in a very explicit way how hard it can be to juggle when these two contexts are combined. As a result, my editor and I decided to address each type of presence across two chapters— one devoted to work and one devoted to home. Communication options change rapidly and norms are continuously evolving, but the concept of social presence—when and where and how to be socially present—persists. And though 2020 gave us all a crash course in many of these ideas, our ability to be thoughtful, strategic, and intentional is critical to success at both work and home. I hope this book helps you to reflect on how you approach your own social presence. And I would love to continue the dialogue with you.

ACKNOWLEDGMENTS

I am grateful to many people in my life who have contributed to my understanding of social presence over the last twenty years. This research has been integrated within most of the courses I have taught at Georgetown University. I began my career at Georgetown in 1997 within the McDonough School of Business, where I had a very applied focus of trying to understand how leaders could communicate more effectively when speaking and writing. After about ten years, I moved to the Graduate School within the CCT Program, where I continued to study communication practices but also tried to explore the theories and frameworks that explain communication processes with graduate students. Having the opportunity to continue to teach in both the business school and the graduate school has kept me simultaneously looking at strategies for how to communicate better and explanations for why those strategies might work.

Specifically, the executive students I have taught within Georgetown's Executive Master's in Business Administration program, Global Executive Master's in Business Administration program, Executive Master's in Leadership Program, the District of Columbia Public Schools' Executive Master's in Leadership Program, and custom executive programs have all helped me to better understand how communication practices have been influenced by the way we use communication technologies to interact. The teams that support these executive programs have been critical to providing me with a landscape for exploring my ideas about presence within the business classroom.

Additionally, within the CCT Program, over the last twelve years, I have taught a graduate-level seminar—Communication Technologies and Organizations—specifically focused on understanding and researching the impact of digital technologies on the way that organizations communicate internally and externally, and I appreciate their insights and support. I have also had the pleasure of working with several graduate research assistants—Adrianne Griffith, Tara Jabbari, Pamela Kaye, Amanda Morris, Katherine Oberkircher, and Fan Wang—who have worked as research assistants and helped gather academic and practitioner literature exploring social presence and the evolving use of communication technologies across a variety of contexts.

My research in cooperation with many other professors has stimulated my thinking in this area. Lamar Reinsch and Catherine Tinsley and I worked together on developing the multicommunicating concept, and Lamar and I have continued with this research. The practice of multicommunicating really stimulated my thoughts and research about presence because it fundamentally changed the way social presence is experienced. My research with Michael O'Leary exploring multitasking continues to help me understand how multicommunicating fits within multitasking and teams. Leticia Bode, Bob Bies, Diana Owen, Pietra Rivoli, Danny Robinson, Keri Stephens, and William Watters have been helpful to me by talking through my ideas, and I really appreciate their insights. Father David McCuland and Father John Dardis helped me to think through how Saint Ignatius of Loyola's ideas concerning communal discernment connected with invitational presence. I would also like to thank Bishop Brian Farrell for his ideas about the impact of presence on ecumenical dialogue. And thanks to Karen Kranack, Jenn McCann, Laurie Mitchell, Tonya Puffett, and Jerry Schmitz for reviewing drafts of these chapters and for their continuous encouragement and support.

Hundreds of individuals and several organizations that I can't name here have contributed their time and ideas about the way they experience social presence to the many stories and examples that provide support for the four types of attentional social presence that I discuss.

About ten years ago, I reached out to my friend Sonja Foss and discussed my ideas about presence with her. These conversations started a collaboration and friendship that has been central to my understanding of presence. My interest in communication technology use and her expertise in rhetoric have contributed to a wonderful partnership, resulting in a stream of research that supports the framework I discuss in this book.

I would also like to thank the director of Georgetown University Press, Al Bertrand; my editor, Hilary Claggett; and Caroline Crossman, Elizabeth Crowley Webber, and the rest of the press's staff for their assistance, support, and encouragement throughout the publishing process.

The idea of social presence is something I consider every day when I am interacting. I think about it when a conversation goes well, but even more when one doesn't go well or doesn't really happen. As a result, some of the people I have talked with the most about social presence—especially during the COVID-19 pandemic, as I was finishing this book—are the members of my family. My parents and my sisters, Nicolette and Michelle, and my sister-in-law Barb have heard more about this concept than they will ever want to know and have continued to listen. My husband, John, and my children—Michael, Kate, and Andrew—have not only modeled every type of social presence on a daily basis but have also been an incredible source of love and support. They remind me every day how critical it is for us to reflect on our social presence and the relationships we are trying to build with every conversation.

Introduction

What Does Social Presence Mean, and Why Should You Care about It?

On March 11, 2020, Georgetown University sent out a message to all the faculty announcing that beginning the following Monday, we would be moving to a "virtual learning environment" and that "all in-person, face-to-face, on-campus classroom instruction would be suspended until further notice."[1] Meanwhile, during the same week, my oldest son received a similar message: that he needed to be picked up from his college in Georgia to return home to finish the semester online. And my daughter and son's high school reported that they would also be moving to online instruction. Within one week's time, we were all trying to use the house's telecommunication infrastructure to create four distinct "learning environments." These changes were felt globally as organizations, communities, and families shifted away from in-person physical interaction where possible, with the home becoming a hub for communication activity.

This collision of work and home, of moving all aspects of our life to the physical confines of our house, created a profound change in our sense of what it meant to be "socially present." I have been studying social presence for over the last thirty years. During this time, I have explored distance education, telemedicine, and telework and how the communication environments could replicate or support the cues and context necessary to help the participants involved to feel as if they were in the same physical space and sharing the same social presence. However, each of these experiments with online communication came embedded within a physical infrastructure where the online component was often a supplement or an added feature. In the spring of 2020, the online environment became the primary means for many people to work, take courses, meet friends, and order food and supplies. The term *social distancing* became important, emphasizing the need to maintain at least 6 feet of space from another person so as to not risk potential contamination from the airborne virus COVID-19.

But I don't need to tell you this. You lived it. No matter where you were living throughout the world, you had to somehow address this complex and unprecedented challenge. So you understand what social distancing means. This book explores *social presence*. While the 2020 pandemic provided new ways to understand how social presence is developed and fostered, the definition of social presence has not changed. The pandemic gave us the opportunity to reflect on the type of presence that occurs when we are in the same room and what it means to have that presence removed. How do you engage your audience? How can you get someone to focus on you? What strategies work when you have status, such as if you are a supervisor or a parent? What strategies work when you don't? This book explores ways to think about the type of presence you are trying to achieve and provides tools to help you achieve those.

WHAT DOES SOCIAL PRESENCE MEAN?

Social presence describes your feeling of being connected within a specific conversation or interaction. Social presence is created by you and your audience. Each person in the conversation contributes to how present you might feel at any moment.[2] For many years, the goal or "gold standard" during mediated conversation has been compared with the presence you might feel if you were physically present, face-to-face. Obviously, in person, physical presence does not guarantee undivided attention and connection. But this standard drove the assessment of communication technology use and its ability to replicate the face-to-face experience.

Your Sense of Social Presence Changes with Use of Different Technologies

While social presence has evolved through many iterations since its first development within the context of the landline telephone, the perception or feeling of being connected with the other person within the context of the conversation has persisted. Some research has explored specific technologies and the extent to which their characteristics lead to a feeling of social presence. For example, some researchers have studied the "richness" of the media, or the number of cues available to convey social presence.[3] A telephone call, which provides for audio cues and immediate feedback, is potentially richer than an email, which provides only textual cues and the feedback is not immediate. Videoconferencing would be considered richer than the phone because of the addition of visual cues, making it closer to replicating a perceived gold standard of face-to-face, in-person social presence.

Researchers have suggested that successful managers would choose rich media for confusing or ambiguous messages and lean or less rich media for messages that were more routine in nature.[4] For example, if you wanted to discuss a complicated client agreement, it would be best to choose a face-to-face meeting. In contrast, if you were going to inform your team about a change in meeting time from 3:00 to 3:30, you might send out a generic email to everyone. These different channels of communication were considered by researchers as a type of container that the message comes in. To be a good communicator, you need to choose the right container.

Social Presence Is Also about Where You Are

However, the match between the message and the communication technology is not the only contributor to decision choices around social presence. Sometimes you can't be there in person. In many ways, the COVID-19 pandemic revealed factors that contribute to social presence that can be taken for granted. At Georgetown University, the classroom conversation is not just influenced by the interaction in the room between a professor and a student. This interaction is influenced by the students' walk from their dorm to the classroom past historic old buildings, the smells and sounds of the campus, the arrangement of chairs in the room, sounds within the building, and the attention and energy of other students in the classroom—and this is before the professor even walks into the room. Turning on a video monitor to see a bunch of faces with unique backgrounds in a video gallery of squares is not the same. And students and faculty tuned in from very different physical contexts. Tuning in to a class from a large monitor, in a comfortable chair, in a quiet room, with a strong Wi-Fi connection, in the same time zone as the class, is not the same as tuning in to a class from the back seat of a car (the only private place in the house that can still connect to the Wi-Fi), in the middle of winter, on a phone, in a time zone that is 8 hours earlier. The environment is consistently in negotiation with the priorities and capabilities of the communicators when making communication choices that lead to social presence.[5]

Social Presence Is Also about Who You Are With

Your relationship with the people in your conversation contributes to your sense of social presence. Certain people can convey more presence in a message based on the relationship you share with them. You might receive a one-word text from a close friend that makes you feel more present and closer to that friend than a long phone conversation with someone else. Or you might notice that some people are great communicating over email but not so great face-to-face. My sister, Nicolette, was one of the first online librarians who worked on a 24/7 chat service providing research assistance to people all over the world in 2000.[6] She developed a voice and comfort with online communication to such an extent that I would often feel more connected with her online than when we talked on the phone. I have seen this as well with my children, nieces, and nephews with texting. In addition to comfort with specific technologies, some people need more time to process messages and can be better at communicating their presence over email than in the quick back-and-forth of face-to-face conversation.[7]

The norms of the other communicators involved can also contribute to the social presence created.[8] In a videoconference, the norms within an organization established by a supervisor regarding whether you turn on your video in a meeting contribute to how socially present communicators feel in that meeting. You might have seen this difference if you ever had the chance to present on an audio call versus presenting on a video call to an audience where they can see you but you can't see them. The social presence you feel is very different in these two situations.

Social Presence Is Also Influenced by What You Are Talking about

In addition to the technologies, the context, and the people involved, the message also can contribute to your sense of social presence. If a message is boring or disturbing, it can alienate the individuals involved. Or if the members of a group of people have a shared experience, a message can feel more socially present. My research with online breast cancer support groups found that individuals with breast cancer found more supportive messages concerning their breast cancer from their online community than they did from their significant other or partner.[9] In this way, the relationship with the person and the content of the message connected to the feeling of presence and connection. Some people say they would rather receive a sensitive or difficult message over an audio connection rather than video so that they are not distracted by the visual cues.

Nonverbal cues make up a large part of our communication message and comprise a huge part of what we miss visually during some forms of mediated interaction. These cues not only provide insights to help you understand the message but also help you to decide whether a message is true.[10] Emojis and emoticons are used to try to make up for the lack of nonverbal messages within the confines of text. Additionally, how fast a person responds to your text can be interpreted as a nonverbal cue. During the pandemic, the use of masks blocked much of your face as you interacted outside your home. Similarly, the inability to shake hands or touch was felt deeply by families, friends, and colleagues and exacerbated a feeling of a lack of presence.[11] These nonverbal cues are so essential to communication that early researchers referred to theories concerning communication media that used text only as "cues filtered out" and cautioned against their ability to develop relationships.[12] However, recent research reveals that while the social presence created through text-only contexts is different from channels with more cues available, these messages contribute to strong relationships, which are sometimes stronger than face-to-face relationships.[13]

Research is also exploring how social presence can be created with avatars or artificial intelligence, and a major emphasis is on nonverbal cues. Some online environments or virtual simulations can feel so real that the individual forgets that they are not communicating with an actual person. A great example of the evolving nature of social presence can be found in an avatar named Ellie created by scientists at the University of Southern California's Institute for Creative Technologies. Patients suffering from posttraumatic stress disorder connect with Ellie over video. Using a computer program that looks for subtle changes in nonverbal gestures and movements, scientists have developed an avatar that could be arguably more responsive than an actual human. As patients talk about their challenges and concerns or past experiences, they receive appropriate positive reinforcement and nonverbal support from Ellie. Ellie is never distracted or upset or frustrated by the conversation. By accessing thousands of measurements of her interviewees (tone, inflection, body language, vocal hesitations, etc.), Ellie is able to respond to the unique needs of each patient, giving the perception of social presence with another human being.[14] Ellie appears to nod her head at the appropriate time, to ask the right questions based on the needs of the patient, and to say the right thing. She provides an interesting example of the intense and complicated way that messaging contributes to your sense of social presence.

While your head may be swimming with all the complexity surrounding the term "social presence," I am now complicating the discussion of social presence even further by turning to the challenge created by your ubiquitous and always-on mobile device.

WHAT HAPPENS WHEN YOU ARE TRYING TO BE PRESENT IN TWO PLACES?

All our discussion of social presence has relied on understanding social presence by considering one conversation at a time. However, with the mobile devices you carry with you everywhere you go, you can actually now be in multiple conversations at once. Have you ever been on an audio conference call while you were also texting someone? Have you been on a web conference where participants are not visible and checked your email? Are you checking your phone while you are reading this right now? Then you are a multicommunicator. Most of us are. Any time you engage in multiple, near-simultaneous conversations at once, you are multicommunicating.[15] You might wonder how this is different from multitasking. Multicommunicating is a type of multitasking involving the very challenging activity of managing messages, relationships, and roles.

Multicommunicating was primarily enabled by the smartphone.[16] The ubiquitous nature of this digital device means that most people carry with them at all times a means for being reached anytime and anywhere. The phone was no longer tied to a landline in terms of restricting physical space, and this same device provided access to both emails, texts, and social media updates. With so many mechanisms for both synchronous (at the same time) and asynchronous (not at the same time) communication, the likelihood of being in one conversation and being interrupted by another became more and more likely. Similarly, the opportunity to start another conversation when bored or distracted during a current conversation became a tempting diversion.

My colleagues and I began discussing the concept of multicommunicating in 2000.[17] The reason I remember the time frame so vividly is that I can recall one of the early conversations that I had with a colleague, while I was also on maternity leave with my first son, Michael. Michael was about six months old, and I remember I had him in a jumpy seat that hung from the door jamb, keeping him contained so that I could also be on the conference call. I was trying to make faces with him to keep him distracted while I was talking on the phone. Case in point, multicommunicating is not new. It does not require a smartphone. So what is different now?

The digitally connected environment around us has introduced more communication channels. Mobile technology has spread rapidly globally, and estimates in 2019 suggested that more than 5 billion people have mobile devices, with half of these connections made via a smartphone.[18] In fact, about a quarter of adults in the United States say they are "almost constantly" online.[19] Online has evolved from carrying a device around to wearing digital devices that allow communication connections to be attached to our bodies. As a result, you never have to miss a phone call or message, and you never have to be stuck in a boring conversation or meeting. Your ability to make choices about how and with whom you are socially present with is unprecedented.

The smartphone introduced a powerful device into all our conversations, whether we were actively using it or not. Now, physical, in-person presence could be easily interrupted by a message from someone else or by you instigating another conversation. And with this incredible capability, the battle for attention was dramatically increased. Once we start carrying a digital device with us everywhere we go, we are navigating between different relationships and conversations all the time. Not only that, the people with whom you are talking are also juggling conversations.[20] So now, if you want to enter into a conversation with someone, you must find a way to get their attention away from whatever conversation that they are already in because you are constantly competing with the distraction of someone's mobile device.

This book explores the impact of multicommunication on the development of social presence. It introduces a framework, based on fifteen years of research and hundreds of interviews, that will help to guide you in understanding how to navigate the challenges of developing social presence in a time of digital distraction.[21]

WHAT IMPACT DOES MULTICOMMUNICATING HAVE ON SOCIAL PRESENCE?

The explosion of communication technology options and types of interaction—from interpersonal to more of a mass audience context through social media—created new norms and expectations for how communication technologies are used and chosen. There are more opportunities for near-simultaneous conversations via text, voice messages, email, social media, and the like, and the frequency with which these opportunities are presented to you has exploded and changed the nature of social presence. As a result, you need to make regular and almost continual choices about the kinds of social presence to construct in a multicommunicative environment. The power of the smartphone continues to evolve with deeper integration into our daily lives with the addition of other applications. Bank applications, home monitoring, shopping, and other transactions send you alerts and notifications that integrate within your life and combine to create a significant attraction to the device and a compelling distraction to your social presence.

HOW ARE NORMS FOR SOCIAL PRESENCE CHANGING?

I have been teaching executive education at Georgetown University for over twenty years. Over this time, I have seen an evolving norm around the use of communication technology in the classroom. I remember sitting in faculty meetings in the business school in the late 1990s where we argued about the importance of bringing laptops into the classroom. About seven years later, we were arguing about the importance of getting laptops out of the classroom to remove the distraction. When the COVID-19 pandemic shut down all in-person, on-campus classes in March 2020, the inability to control students' use of technology became immediately obvious (some would argue it was never possible), especially since students were connecting to the university with the very technology that would connect them to email, social media, and texting distractions. While I experienced this shift in the university environment, similar shifts and recognition of the evolving power of the audience were being recognized in other industries. How can I get my audience to pay attention and listen? How can I guarantee undivided attention?

Did People Ever Pay Attention?

As individuals had access to a technology that allowed them to connect anywhere and anytime to anyone, they were faced with a choice about where they wanted to be socially present. Digital technologies create the opportunity for you to feel like you can be present in multiple environments at once. But research says you can't truly multitask, much less multicommunicate.[22] This divided attention can lead to a disengaged audience.

And obviously, digital devices are not the sole cause of a disengaged audience. People have always pretended to pay attention in class. Since kindergarten and circle time, you learn to look at the teacher and act like you care about what she is saying as a sign of respect. You didn't necessarily give her your attention; you could have been thinking about many things. But your nonverbal cues probably suggested that you were paying attention.

Over the past twenty years, I have seen students move from pretending to pay attention, to trying to hide their digital devices while they pretended to pay attention, to not pretending at all and not trying to hide their devices at all. When all classes moved online during the pandemic, I had fewer cues about my students' attention. Students could turn off their camera and be listening but be having bandwidth issues, or they could turn off their camera and be watching Netflix. Students could appear to be looking off to the side because of their camera placement or because they were reading email. Students in classrooms and employees in virtual meetings and family members on a video call had more agency than ever before to make decisions about whether to give you their full, undivided attention.

In fact, many individuals don't see divided attention between two conversations as a problem but more as an opportunity. Additionally, many people privilege the presence of the conversation on their digital device rather than the in-person conversation. I was conducting a focus group of mostly students and a few professors about the impact of communication technologies and multicommunicating on the classroom environment. One professor lamented that laptops in the classroom were not the only problem and told the story of a male student in her 300-person science lecture who had a newspaper with him that he was holding up in a distracting way during the class. She tried to suggest to him subtly a number of times to put the newspaper away, but he ignored her. Finally, she asked him to put it away and he actually came to her office later and complained that she had embarrassed him in the class. But this isn't the oddest part of this story. While the professor was retelling this story, a freshman woman sitting next to me became more and more visibly upset by the rude behavior of this male student in the story. I was surprised that she was upset, considering she had spent the last 40 minutes of the focus group glued to her iPad, generally appearing to ignore the conversation. I finally said, "I have to ask. You are appalled by this student's behavior, yet you have been sitting in this focus group for the past 40 minutes glued to your iPad. How is that different than the student in the science class?" She was incredulous, "My behavior isn't rude. My iPad gives me up-to-the-minute information and is constantly keeping me up to date with the information that I need. His newspaper is at least 24 hours old." So her definition of being fully present included not just her physical presence in a classroom but also being fully present in the contextual world around her. Our focus group was one of many messages she was juggling and managing as she monitored changes in the world around her. This story reinforces the justification many people make as to the importance of immediacy and real-time interaction.

Another example of the importance of immediacy and rapid feedback provided by multicommunicating and the ability to allocate or distribute presence came from a principal who was a student in one of the executive programs where I teach. A principal of a middle school described that he had his smartphone with him and on at all times. In fact, he argued that when he is in a face-to-face conversation with a parent and his phone rings, he pauses the face-to-face conversation and takes the phone call. "Wow! Why do you do that?" I asked, thinking of the many conversations I have had myself with principals or teachers about my children and wondering about his rationale for this approach. He responded, "I want that parent that I am talking with face-to-face to know that if he calls me on the phone, I will answer as well." In both of these examples, face-to-face is no longer primary but secondary to the smartphone or digital device being carried.

These changing norms are especially challenging because of the speed with which they are changing and the variety of capabilities available on a mobile device.[23] The smartphone is a complicated device and the norms that define how you use your device are unique, making shared norms across huge groups of people almost impossible.[24] Executives tell me about global conference calls that have gone on for three days, with people taking turns on the call. Other managers brag about the number of meetings that they can attend at once. Simultaneously, businesspeople and academics lament the lack of attention by students and individuals in their meetings, conversations, or classrooms.

Your audience has the power to choose to attend. When your organization moved online in March 2020 during the pandemic, your audience had more choice about how to be socially present than ever before. Now they can choose to turn their camera on or off, depending on how visible they want to be. They can turn their audio on or off, depending on whether they want you to be able to hear them.

So how can you make decisions about where and when to be socially present?

WHAT HAS BEEN THE ADVICE TO DATE?

Just turn off your phone/laptop/digital device. This advice suggests that individuals take the time to focus on one thing at a time. Multitasking research suggests that you can't actually multitask productively.[25] Some research has argued that people have become addicted to their devices and that, for their own good, you need to remove their technology from them so that they can benefit from your meeting or conversation.[26] So most of the advice has been binary—either turn your devices on and multicommunicate, or turn them off. While it is true that that choice is available to you, the strategy behind turning off your devices and the costs and benefits associated with your decisions about where you will be socially present is missing from the current conversation about presence. Within our networked and always-on environment, "just turn it off" is a rather simplistic approach to a very complex problem.[27]

Organizations are trying to be creative and often create competitions. People regularly tell me about the basket that is put in the center of a table to collect phones at work until the meeting is over. Others have described situations at a restaurant where everyone puts their phones in the center of the table and the first person to reach for their phone has to pay the bill. Some organizations have created four-hour windows where individuals cannot use their phones. Countries have instituted policies where employees cannot send work-related emails over the weekend.[28] People talk about giving up their phone for Lent. One company asks employees to keep track of phone usage, and at the end of the day, all employees report phone use on a whiteboard. The person who has used their phone the least gets some sort of prize. There seems to be widespread recognition of a problem that needs to be addressed.

Most of the strategies that I have heard or read about involve completely turning the phone off, or physically removing the phone from one's reach, for a specific period.[29] Sherry Turkle, a professor at the Massachusetts Institute of Technology, has spent years exploring the impact of technology on our relationships. She makes an impassioned and critical plea in her book *Reclaiming Conversation* for the importance of engaging in focused interaction—but how do we do that? Turning off our devices seems more and more unrealistic.[30]

Because you have the potential to be ubiquitously available, the expectation by many of the networks of people in your life has greatly increased that you will be "responsive" to messages. Sometimes it seems that the rate with which a person responds to your message communicates the level of intimacy or importance of the relationship. This capability puts even greater pressure on you to respond. You walk around connected to family networks, neighborhood networks, work networks, school networks, friend networks, and logistical or operational networks. Any one of these networks could experience perceived or real emergencies where your input or advice is needed. In my classes, some people argue that they never used to need to be available every minute of the day, so why has that changed? The difference is that you didn't need to be available because you couldn't be. Unless you were near a rotary phone or someone with a phone like that who could contact you, you couldn't be reached. People would sometimes stay home or stay in their office waiting for a phone call. Now there is an expectation by all the networks that you are a part of that you will be able to be reached. This expectation changes everything. You often can't afford to put your phone away for a long period, but you still need to be mindful about how you use your mobile devices and how you communicate your social presence.

WHAT SHOULD WE DO ABOUT THE PRESSURE TO MULTICOMMUNICATE?

I suggest that you need to think critically and strategically about the communication situations that you are in on a minute-by-minute basis and analyze the costs and benefits of your social presence decisions as they relate to the management of your messages and your relationships. This means that you actually have four possible options as a communicator as you decide about how best to convey your social presence—budgeted presence, entitled presence, competitive presence, and invitational presence:

Attentional presence choices	What does it mean?
Budgeted	You triage your presence while managing multiple conversations.
Entitled	You control other people's presence by taking their device away.

Competitive   You compete for your audience's
                       attention from their devices with the
                       goal of persuasion.
Invitational   You invite your audience into a
                       conversation with the goal of learning
                       but not controlling presence.

Budgeted Presence

Budgeted social presence is probably your default state these days, and it describes a communicative state where you are managing multiple conversations at once. You are paying part of your attention to me and part to other digital devices available to you. Here, you are focused on your own availability as you juggle and manage messages by allocating partial attention to each interaction. You treat your audience as an expenditure, and you are always evaluating how much of your attention this person or group is worth.

Entitled Presence

Entitled social presence is a second presence option for you, and here you try to control the environment and have your audience focus only on you. You limit messages so that your audience receives only your message. For example, you might ask someone to put their phone away or down and listen to you. With this strategy, you are treating your audience as a container.

Competitive Presence

In competitive social presence, you hope to influence your audience to attend only to your message. However, instead of trying to remove your audience's distractions, you compete with your audience's messages by using persuasive strategies to win their attention. Here, you treat your audience as an investor.

Invitational Presence

Finally, with invitational social presence, you hope to create a partnership with your audience. You are creating a dialogue and focusing only on this one conversation, but you are not making requirements of your audience. Rooted in the theory of invitational rhetoric, here you invite your audience into your conversation by trying to understand their perspective and share yours.[31] Here, you treat your audience as a partner.

A USEFUL FRAMEWORK FOR INTENTIONAL COMMUNICATION

These options make up a framework I created with my colleague Sonja Foss that communicators can use when making social presence decisions.[32] While I am arguing that social presence is a decision one person makes, this decision is obviously embedded within a conversation or a group of conversations. Communication is a complicated and complex process that is co-created by two or more individuals in a reciprocal way on an ongoing basis. At any one time, one person is the communicator and the other is the responder. But it is not even as linear as that. While one person is talking, the other person is enacting a response and reading nonverbal and verbal cues to inform that response. So taking a snapshot of any one moment in time and identifying the communicator, listener, and degrees of social presence might seem unrealistic. However, this snapshot is a place to start. And with this attention to social presence on a minute-by-minute basis, you can become more strategic and intentional in the way that you manage your social presence. While in a meeting, when a mobile device vibrates, what questions should guide the decision to engage and which social presence matters more?

While communicators have always needed to gain the attention of the audience, the mediated, "always-on" environment means that part of your communication strategy has to involve attention to how you will explicitly address the communication devices in the room. I describe this as attentional social presence.[33] Attentional presence starts with the need to engage your audience in some way and then choose the type of control that makes the most sense for the type of social presence you want to achieve.

HOW CAN YOU EXPLORE THESE STRATEGIES IN THE BOOK?

In this book, I explore in more detail these four types of social presence that are available to any communicator at any moment. In the following chapters, I examine each strategy as it relates to work as well as how it relates to situations outside of work, like family, friends, and school. While the work and home environments are often intertwined, their relationships and priorities can be very different. As a result, I have separated work and home/family/friendships/school to help you tease through the very different dynamics in these two contexts. I include many examples from my experience teaching in the university and some classroom examples from outside the university. Whether or not you are taking courses now, you have had classroom experience and can use these examples to understand how different presentation strategies play out in different contexts. The goal of this book is to provide you with insights toward creating a more intentional and strategic approach to the context, the individuals involved, and the messaging when making your presence choices.

You will be introduced to the specifics of each type of presence in the next chapters. Chapters 2 and 3 explore budgeted presence within work and at home, where your focus is on allocating your presence in the most efficient way possible. Budgeted presence is often our default state, and then we move to one of the other choices when we attempt to control our audience. Chapters 4 and 5 examine entitled presence—first at work and then at home. In these two chapters, I explore the choice you make when you are trying to control the technology of your audience as a means of keeping their attention. Chapters 6 and 7 explore competitive presence at work and at home. Here, the focus is on trying to compete for the attention of your audience by making a persuasive message. In chapters 8 and 9, I discuss invitational presence at work and at home. With invitational presence, you are choosing to have a dialogue with your audience and

REFLECTION EXERCISE

- How often do you turn off your phone during a conversation or meet-ing, and what are the driving factors that influence this decision?
- Who are the people in your life that generally "earn" a focused and undivided conversation with you?
- What topics of conversation make sense for a focused and undivided conversation?
- When does it seem most appropriate to engage in multiple conversations at once?
- How does your visibility and whether your conversational partners can detect whether you are multicommunicating affect your decision to engage in multiple conversations at once?
- When do you feel most socially present?

treat them as a partner in the conversation. Finally, in chapter 10 we conclude with strategies for addressing the situation when you choose one type of presence and your audience chooses a different type. I describe each of these strategies for you to consider when faced with needing to gain the audience's attention, the view the communicator has of the audience when using that type of attentional social presence, and the costs and benefits of choosing that strategy. Throughout the book and at the end of each chapter, I offer exercises and points of reflection to help you to apply these ideas into your own life.

Before we go on, think about how you use your digital device. Answer the reflection questions above and make notes. Then move on to read the next chapters and learn about the social presence choices that are available to you and what they mean for the type of social presence you are trying to construct.

NOTES

1. Office of the President, Georgetown University, "Letter to Members of the Georgetown Community," March 11, 2020.

2. John Short, Ederyn Williams, and Bruce Christie, *The Social Psychology of Telecommunications* (New York: John A. Wiley & Sons, 1976).

3. Richard Daft and Robert Lengel, "Organization Requirements, Media Richness, and Structural Design," *Organization Design* 32, no. 5 (1986): 554–71, doi:10 .1287/mnsc.32.5.554.

4. Daft and Lengel.

5. Ronald Rice, "Task Analyzability, Use of New Media, and Effectiveness: A Multi-site Exploration of Media Richness," *Organization Science* 3, no. 4 (1992): 475–500, doi:10.1287/orsc.3.4.475.

6. Library of Congress, *Reference 24/7: Libraries Test Collaborative Digital Reference Service* (Washington, DC: Library of Congress, 2020), loc.gov/loc/lcib/0010 /ref.html.

7. Rich Ling and Scott W. Campbell, eds., *The Reconstruction of Space and Time: Mobile Communication Practices* (New Brunswick, NJ: Transaction, 2010).

8. John Carlson and Robert W. Zmud, "Channel Expansion Theory and the Experiential Nature of Media Richness Perceptions," *Academy of Management Journal* 42, no. 2 (1999): 153–70, doi.org/10.2307/257090.

9. Jeanine Warisse Turner, Jean A. Grube, and Jennifer Meyers, "Developing an Optimal Match within Online Communities: An Exploration of CMC Support Communities and Traditional Support," *Journal of Communication* 51, no. 2 (2001): 231–51.

10. Leanne Brinke and Max Weisbuch, "How Verbal-Nonverbal Consistency Shapes the Truth," *Journal of Experimental Social Psychology* 89 (2020): 103978.

11. Shanley Pierce, "Touch Starvation Is a Consequence of COVID-19's Physical Distancing," Texas Medical Center, May 2020, tmc.edu/news/2020/05/touch-star vation/.

12. Lee Sproull and Sara Kiesler, *Connections: New Ways of Working in the Networked Organization* (Cambridge, MA: MIT Press, 1991).

13. Joseph Walther, "Computer-Mediated Communication: Impersonal, Interpersonal, and Hyperpersonal Interaction," *Communication Research* 23, no. 1 (1996): 3–43.

14. Alix Spiegel, "If Your Shrink Is a Bot, How Do You Respond?" NPR: Your Health, May 20, 2013, www.npr.org/sections/health-shots/2013/05/20/182593855 /if-your-shrink-is-a-bot-how-do-you-respond.

15. N. Lamar Reinsch Jr., Jeanine Warisse Turner, and Catherine H. Tinsley, "Multicommunicating: A Practice Whose Time Has Come?" *Academy of Management Review* 33, no. 2 (2008): 391–403.

16. Reinsch, Turner, and Tinsley.

17. Reinsch, Turner, and Tinsley.

18. Laura Silver, "Smartphone Ownership Is Growing Rapidly around the World, but Not Always Equally," Pew Research Center: Global Attitudes and Trends,

February 5, 2019, www.pewresearch.org/global/2019/02/05/smartphone-owner
ship-is-growing-rapidly-around-the-world-but-not-always-equally/.

19. Andrew Perrin and Madhu Kumar, "About Three in 10 US Adults Say They
Are 'Almost Constantly' Online," Pew Research Center, March 14, 2018, www.pew
research.org/fact-tank/2018/03/14/about-a-quarter-of-americans-report-going-on
line-almost-constantly/.

20. Ann Cameron, Henri Barki, Ana Ortiz de Guinea, Thibaut Coulon, and
Hanieh Moshki, "Multicommunicating in Meetings: Effects of Locus, Topic Re-
latedness, & Meeting Medium," *Management Communication Quarterly* 32, no. 3
(2018): 303–36.

21. Jeanine Warisse Turner and Sonja K. Foss, "Options for the Construction of
Social Presence in a Digitally Enhanced Multicommunicative Environment," *Communication Theory* 28, no. 1 (2018): 22–45, doi:10.1093/ct/qty002.

22. Cynthia Kubu and Andre Mcahado, "The Science Is Clear: Why Multitasking Doesn't Work: We Really Can't Do Two Things at Once." Cleveland Clinic: Brain
and Spine, June 1, 2017, http://health.clevelandclinic.org/science-clear-multitask
ing-doesn't-work/.

23. Keri Stephens and Jennifer Davis, "The Social Influences on Electronic
Multitasking in Organizational Meetings," *Management Communication Quarterly*
23, no. 1 (2009): 63–83.

24. Rushika De Bruin and Larissa Barber, "Social Judgments of Electronic Multitasking in the Workplace: The Role of Contextual and Individual Factors," *Computers in Human Behavior* 94 (2019): 110–21.

25. Constance Holden, "Multitasking: Bad for the Brain?" *Science* 325, no. 5944
(August 28, 2009): 1053, doi:10.1126/science.325_1053bd.

26. Cristian Jenaro, Noelia Flores, Maria Gómez-Vela, Francisca González-Gil,
and Cristina Caballo, "Problematic Internet and Cellphone Use: Psychological,
Behavioral, and Health Correlates," *Addiction Research & Theory* 15, no. 3 (2007):
309–20, doi:10.1080/16066350701350247.

27. Emily Paskewitz and Stephenson Beck, "'Put the Phone Away!' Does Text
Message Content Influence Perceptions of Group Member Texting?" *Computers in
Human Behavior* 115 (2021): 106591, https://doi.org/10.1016/j.chb.2020.106591.

28. David Morris, "New French Law Bars Work Email After Hours," *Fortune*,
January 1, 2017, https://fortune.com/2017/01/01/French-right-to-disconnect-law/.

29. Cal Newport, *Digital Minimalism: Choosing a Focused Life in a Noisy World*
(New York: Penguin, 2019).

30. Sherry Turkle, *Reclaiming Conversation: The Power of Talk in the Digital Age*
(New York: Penguin, 2015).

31. Sonja Foss and Cindy Griffin, "Beyond Persuasion: A Proposal for Invitational Rhetoric," *Communication Monographs* 62, no. 1 (1995): 2–18, doi:10.1080/03637759509376345.

32. Jeanine Warisse Turner and Sonja K. Foss, "Options for the Construction of Social Presence in a Digitally Enhanced Multicommunicative Environment," *Communication Theory* 28, no. 1 (2018): 22–45, doi:10.1093/ct/qty002.

33. Turner and Foss.

Part I

Paying Some Attention, Screens On
Budgeted Presence

You already know what budgeted presence is—in fact, you probably spend most of your waking moments here. Part I describes budgeted presence as "screens on" because your device is on and you are multicommunicating. Read on to understand what this choice might mean for you.

1

Budgeted Presence in the Workplace

Digital devices gave birth to budgeted presence—you are able to give part of your attention to one conversation and part of your attention to another conversation. Just as you budget other resources like money or time to prioritize resources to show what you care about, you are also able to budget your presence. Many people do not create budgets for their finances and come to the end of the month and run out of money because they didn't think about their resources carefully. Similarly, people can reach the end of a day or week without getting major projects finished because time was not managed effectively. You can think about the idea of budgeting when you are thinking of managing your presence with the conversations around you.

The digital device that you carry with you every day allows you to be reached at any time or to reach out to someone else at any time. Sometimes, you might not even realize how many times you glance at your phone during an ongoing conversation. While you might not pay attention to how much time you use your phone, you are probably pretty aware when you are talking with someone and they are distracted by their phone. It can be pretty frustrating. Said one CEO of a technology firm:

> "I was talking with one of my employees, Joe, yesterday and I was so frustrated. He is about 30 years old. Every time he comes into my office, he has his phone out. Not only does he glance at it while I am talking to him, but he sometimes responds! He doesn't even apologize! He just keeps talking to me and acts like I don't know what he is doing. I was fuming!"

"Did you say anything?"

"No. . . . I don't want to seem like I am too old or that I don't
'get technology.' But I will never promote him."

In this example, Joe may not even realize how much he is distracted
by the incoming messages on his mobile device. Additionally, Joe probably does not realize how much he is bothering the CEO. However, this
behavior is likely to cost him his promotion.[1] I use the term "budgeted
presence" to reinforce to communicators that they are making a choice
about where to focus their presence every moment of every day. This
chapter explores what budgeted presence means and the implications of
this choice of attentional social presence.

While communicators have always been able to schedule conversations or meetings, you are now able to switch between meetings and hold
simultaneous meetings with multiple partners across multiple locations.
In the introduction to this book, I described the practice of *multicommu-*
nicating. Budgeted presence is the name of the presence you are choosing
when you have decided to multicommunicate. Let's explore the implications of this choice and the intentional (and unintentional) impact it has
on your tasks and relationships.

WHAT IS BUDGETED PRESENCE?

Budgeted presence happens when you are in at least two separate conversations at the same time. Budgeted presence can also happen when you
are in a conversation with one person and your phone vibrates or rings
to indicate that another message is coming in. In fact, some research has
shown that just the visible presence of a phone—the potential for multicommunication—can have an impact on the conversation. Merely having
your phone available and continually glancing at your phone may have an
impact on the conversations around you.[2]

Some of the research has shown that perspectives are actually evolving over time as people get more and more used to distractions during
conversations. Earlier research found that the presence of a smartphone

Review of Budgeted Presence

Type of Presence	View of Audience	Goal	Benefits	Costs
Budgeted	Expenditure	Efficient management of messages	Accomplish tasks	Potential norm infractions and diminished relationship development

influenced the way conversational partners relationally viewed the interaction. Initially, people reported being upset when a conversational partner glanced at their mobile device. Later studies have not found the same degree of concern or frustration but rather a resigned acceptance of this behavior.[3] Changing norms have been cited as a possible explanation—and I am not surprised. As I continue to talk with people about the use of digital devices, I find a very complicated relationship between perceptions of mobile phone use and conversations. Norms are shifting.

As one executive shared with me, "It doesn't really bother me when someone is on their phone while I am talking to them. I guess I expect that. What bothers me is when they are looking bored while I am talking or looking off into the distance. That really bothers me." Where it used to appear rude to be interacting with a mobile device while in a face-to-face conversation, this action is now often expected. But looking off into the distance and not being engaged in anything? Now that is rude. We now explore evolving norms that contribute to the growth of budgeted presence.

The Norm That Multicommunicating Is Increasingly Acceptable

Budgeted presence—with the increasing acceptance of the practice of multicommunicating—has also become increasingly accepted, whether in meetings or interpersonal conversations. Much like an air traffic controller, you are constantly making decisions about where and when messages should land around you. Realistically, with the diffusion of digital devices, you find yourself in budgeted presence most of the day. Digital devices allow you to efficiently manage your availability across multiple message streams. You never need to waste time in a conversation that seems to be going nowhere because you have a device with you that allows you to connect to a relevant conversation. Your own attention becomes a resource that you manage carefully, regardless of the feelings of the people around you. You don't want to waste your attention on conversations that are not worth it. One executive director of a large nonprofit agency talked about the importance of staying in budgeted presence: "I am probably on my phone too much. But I have to stay connected in case someone in the organization needs me. I am pretty sure I know when I need to be dialed in to the meetings I am in and when I don't. I can just tell. I can get so much done because I never have to waste time in a meeting."

The Norm That Content Must Be Relevant

I continuously hear that people are concerned that we are addicted to our technologies. Some people raise the concern that we can't stop ourselves. Many executives in my classes in the executive degree program, or in the custom programs I teach with executives, have suggested that we are giving ourselves ADHD. While some people might be addicted to their technology, I don't think that digital addiction is necessarily the concern facing the majority of the population.[4] However, I do think people are unaware of how much they use their mobile devices.

You are often reacting to your devices rather than being intentional in your behavior vis-à-vis your devices. You are continuously searching for relevance. This need to be engaged in relevant conversations or information motivates you to continuously troll for the most relevant information available. Relevance can be in the form of important information, entertainment, or both. People have shared with me that they are reluctant to allow a conversation to take a turn that is not seen as productive or relevant. Their access to a digital device helps them to triage their presence across multiple audiences so they can be "available" in the most efficient way. One person I interviewed said, "At my job, I would frequently have multiple conversations. I would discuss research assignments over the phone with my boss, while composing a memo to my other boss about some litigation issue, while instant messaging my friends about how they were doing. I liked the instant messaging because it kept me awake and made the other tasks less 'painful,' but I usually had to direct most of my attention to the phone call."

In addition to searching for relevance on your phones as audience members, you also strive to be relevant to your audience. Your mobile devices provide you with many opportunities for asynchronous messages or messages where you can't see your audience's immediate response. You can imagine the audience; and when you do, you can also imagine them to be interested, laughing, and involved in your conversations.[5] You can't use your imagination in the same way in a synchronous interaction where you can see the person with whom you are talking. Maybe that is why our society has become so engaged with social media. Our "imagined audience" is always paying attention and always cares.[6]

The Norm of Continuous Availability

Anytime you have your digital devices with you, you are engaged in budgeted presence. You may be allocating 95 percent of your presence to one conversation and 5 percent to your phone or device, watching to see if someone else might call. But just that 5 percent means you are less focused on the current conversation. Talking with someone and then glancing down at the phone when it vibrates disrupts the conversation. Even if you decide not to pick up the phone when it vibrates, you are still giving attention to the digital device. One person I talked with joked about the use of BlackBerry devices in the early 2000s, "When I was working in politics, we used to joke that the BlackBerry was just an extension of one's arm. They were the new hand, . . . because you always had to be available. When I first started, they were the ones for emails, but then quite quickly, the dual phone, email, and internet ones were more available. When I went out, even in the hallway or walking somewhere, there was that constant head bent down and scrolling." This experience highlights a trend of availability that spread and has infiltrated most professions and walks of life.

Not only do mobile phones help you be available, they specifically grant greater availability to your most intimate sphere.[7] You can actually be constantly connected to a specified group through a specific app, where throughout the day you continue a conversation with someone or a group of people. Similarly, you can be reachable to everyone who has your mobile numbers. This availability has been called "connected presence."[8] And while this type of availability can add to an increased level of intimacy with the people who are constantly connected but physically separated, these conversations can also serve to interrupt other conversations going on in those physical spaces. One of my interviewees is a high school teacher who talked about the ongoing conversation that she had with a group of friends from college while at work. "We keep our conversation going all day with WhatsApp. We are never not in a conversation. I feel closer to those friends than any of the people that I work with."

Continuous availability can also be leveraged with conference calls across time zones and physical spaces. One government contractor who develops bids for telecommunications work talked about how he has had conference calls go on for days at a time. "One time, we had a conference call that lasted three days. Sometimes people had to step off for other meetings or to eat or sleep. But we had the continuous channel going so that we could get our proposal in."

TOOLS FOR TECHNOLOGICAL TRIAGE

Budgeted presence can spread across a wide variety of availability options. The primary element within budgeted presence is the need to be physically and virtually available in multiple places at any one time. This availability can span a large continuum. For example, you may have your phone turned on and be generally available to any incoming message. This message could come from a retail store with an upcoming discount, a family member with a concern about planning an event, or a colleague with a request for changes on a report. Each one of these outside-work interruptions can pull you away from a current workplace conversation or meeting for seconds or minutes at a time. While you usually cannot anticipate how long this interruption will be, you still often introduce this interruption into your current conversation by checking the message.

Some individuals carefully triage their social presence. They might do this by managing multiple devices or phones. One executive I talked with worked with the White House. For security reasons, he kept a phone for work-related issues and a phone for personal issues. In this way, he may be prioritizing the personal phone because he knows exactly who has that number and therefore privileges it when it indicates an incoming message. Other individuals triage messages through software on their digital device so that only certain messages come through. This management might mean that they have all their messages going to one device but that only a specific group of individuals with special access can leave a message or connect with their smartwatch or alternative device.

These triaging behaviors can help you manage your presence in a more intentional way, but they still create interruptions. I had a conversation with a former student who works with Google. I asked him if there were ever situations where people did not have access to their messages. He responded, "Do you mean going dark? No, we don't go dark at Google." In fact, Google is in the business of keeping us connected, so it is in its best interest to provide triage technology so that these messages are handled in the least obtrusive way.

This triage can come in wearable devices. Wearable devices have made some of the nonverbal cues associated with checking a device subtler. One manager told me she was more relaxed in conversations with her Apple Watch because she could easily glance at it to check a message without having to fumble around in her briefcase, looking for her phone. In fact, she feels that she can be more socially present because she is able to budget so efficiently without disrupting the current conversation. The seamless integration of worn mobile devices helps to mask the messages from the other communicators in the interaction but still serves as an interruption for the person wearing the device.

During the COVID-19 pandemic, when offices moved online and primarily interacted over video, participants found themselves connected to their desktop and their videoconferencing application all day long. When you are on a videoconference, you have the option to turn off your camera. Many people would choose to turn off their camera, turning the video-conference into an audioconference to enable them to multitask during the calls. However, in doing so, they removed their visual presence from the conversation. While your meeting might be more efficient when you make this decision, you need to consider the implications of not show-ing yourself in the meeting and becoming "visually invisible" within the organization.

All these examples point to methods used to budget presence. As technologies become "smarter" and are able to provide more effective triage of your attention, the interruptive nature, or the magnitude of the interruption within budgeted presence, will change. Regardless of how obtrusive the interruption is, the *likelihood* that a person can get a mes-sage during a conversation changes the nature of that conversation. And the interruption of a conversation because of an incoming message can hijack the current conversation and could disrupt the task or upset the relationship. While budgeted presence includes a wide range of interrup-tion opportunities, the single factor of being available to other conversa-tions during a single conversation crosses all examples.

WHO IS YOUR AUDIENCE?

When you adopt budgeted presence, you are viewing your audience as an *expenditure*. Communicators try to allocate their presence in the most efficient way across a variety of audiences. Budgeted presence, through our digital devices, creates an agency for audiences never before seen. No longer do you need to suffer through a time-consuming, irrelevant meet-ing. When studying multicommunicating, I often ask people, "How do you do it? How do you engage in multiple conversations at any one time?" And the answer that I usually get is, "I listen when it pertains to me. Most people can't do it. It can be difficult but I can do it."

So, basically, most people believe they have some type of relevance radar that is constantly scanning the atmosphere for information that matters. I often wonder if it actually is relevance that is being used as a benchmark. Relevance to whom? And are you sure it is relevance? Could it also be that you listen when you agree with your audience? That you listen when you like the person? Or that you listen when the conversation is comfortable? These are very different reasons than relevance. However, your digital devices do not discriminate. These devices are always available to you when you are in a conversation that is uncomfortable, awkward, or boring to save you from your audience. They will save you from those conversations so you never have to be bored or uncomfortable again.

Viewing your audience as an expenditure is very different from viewing your audience as a relationship. When you view the audience as an expenditure, messages become something that can be juggled or managed so that attention balances most efficiently at the end. I often tell executives that we might be able to view our audiences as balls to be juggled if everyone that we talk with likes us and wants to do whatever we want them to do. If your audiences don't need to be persuaded and don't need to have buy-in, then juggling messages or allocating social presence expenditures can work. In fact, the extent to which the audience does not know that they are being viewed as an expenditure—for example, you are on an audio conference call while also texting your friends—budgeted presence may have no impact on the conversation. Budgeted presence doesn't have to hurt a relationship if the audience is unaware or if the audience does not care. Similarly, if the incoming message is routine or simple, it might not need much of your attention or concentration, so budgeted presence can be adequate.

WHERE'S THE FOCUS OF CONTROL IN BUDGETED PRESENCE?

The focus of control with budgeted presence is the control of availability. You are able to use your digital device to make the most efficient decisions possible about your presence. When you effectively employ budgeted presence, you are able to accumulate additional minutes and hours that you would have spent in sequential interactions by engaging in multiple interactions at any one time. In this way, you are able to achieve maximum productivity.

Availability has become an important characteristic. Even more important than availability is avoiding the label "nonresponsive." One executive remarked, "Being labeled unresponsive is the kiss of death. No one wants to be on a team with you, no one wants to have to depend on you. Pretty soon, no one is calling you. And that is much worse." Leslie Perlow, a professor of leadership at the Harvard Business School, has identified this challenge as "the cycle of unresponsiveness."[9] This cycle starts with an individual's pressure to be "always on," followed by a need to make sure she is always accessible, so that people think she can be counted on, so she responds to nonurgent requests to illustrate her availability, and, as a result, she has her digital device with her and on at all times. In this way, your decision to disconnect is not an individual decision but a team decision that must be supported by organizational and interpersonal norms. Budgeted presence is not just an individual choice but also a choice embedded within the expectations of your key audiences that fuels how you approach social presence.

A problem that is similar and closely connected to the responsiveness issue is the practice of escalation. Escalation describes what happens when you are not immediately available to answer a question or concern so your colleague asks your superior or boss. Another interviewee named Steve described escalation in his organization this way: "If I don't reply to a text or email in a reasonable amount of time [the exact time that constituted reasonable was not clear], the person that was contacting me has the right to escalate the issue to a person at a higher level and indicate that I was not responsive." Escalation can create an organization-wide exigency for budgeted presence. Escalation means that not only do some of the people on your team think you are unresponsive, so does your boss.

Thus, you start to focus on your availability. In doing so, you privilege multicommunicating and engage in budgeted social presence. One interviewee who is a male business owner and who was raised in the United States and South Africa talked about budgeted presence in this way: "It happens about 24 hours a day for me. When I am on the speaker phone, I will be texting frequently. I work from home so I have to. More than three [conversations at once] is impossible, three is a challenge." Another executive from a pharmaceutical company described the opportunity provided by budgeted presence: "When I am in a meeting that is unproductive or a presentation that is not relevant to me, I go to my emails and messages to start going through those. I don't feel bad about it. My organization needs me to be productive. If the person leading my meeting or presenting to me is not relevant to me, I need to work on something that is relevant. My organization expects me to manage my productivity in the most efficient way possible."

These examples point to the changing definition of social presence within the work environment. Social presence is measured not within single meetings or conversations but with a balance sheet that looks at social presence as it is spent across the organizations. Every moment needs to balance out with the most efficient use of our attention and social presence.

WHAT ARE THE BENEFITS?

You probably know the benefits of budgeted presence—or imagine its benefits—which is why we all engage in this type of presence most minutes every day. Budgeted presence is becoming a starting space from which all other presence choices are made. People tell me that they actually sleep with their phone under their pillow. While in budgeted presence, you never have to worry about sitting in an irrelevant conversation, meeting, or context. And irrelevant contexts seem to be everywhere. Unfortunately, many business messages are not targeted toward the needs of the audience. You often must attend meetings where you don't understand the point. You ask yourself, "Why were we invited? What value is this to me or what value can I bring to this meeting?" At least having your digital device with you ensures that the hour or session is not a complete waste of time and attention.

Additionally, in your networked environment, where expectation norms for a communication response can be as quick as "within a few minutes," you can be available for your colleagues or project teams in

some decision-making capacity. You can also be available to your children, significant others, family members, and neighbors during work
hours (an ability not so prevalent until the spread of ubiquitous digital
devices). When I ask individuals about successful examples of budgeted
presence, I often get examples where the person was in a large lecture
or meeting that provided "cover" for that multicommunicating behavior.
Other examples include ways that access to other colleagues during a
meeting can contribute to the richness of a specific meeting. One executive actually requires her team to be constantly present in chat during
work hours. She described the situation this way:

> Skype chat is an excellent communications tool for me and I tell my
> team I want them to be present on Skype for chat whether they're work-
> ing from home, or in the office. That way, if I am on a conference call
> and let's say that someone is asking a question of something that they
> didn't have the answer right away, but I know someone on our team has
> the answer, I send them like a quick message like, "Hey, X, & and Z,"
> whatever. And I get the answer right away and then I can go back at the
> same call and tell them, "Hey, the answer is," rather than, "Oh, I'll get
> back to you later," kind of thing.

Other benefits of budgeted presence are best realized when you are
not visible to your communicators, as when you are on a web conference
or audio call. In fact, because of the efficiencies provided by budgeted
presence, people are often reticent to schedule synchronous encounters.
You may find yourself avoiding face-to-face meetings or telephone interactions. The very act of being in a synchronous, and especially face-to-
face, encounter necessarily limits your options for multicommunicating
and can almost hold you captive in a setting that is or becomes irrelevant.[10]
One government employee talked about her budgeted presence strategy
on conference calls: "I routinely engage in multiple conversations at once
while I am on a conference call. Then if someone asks me a question, I
usually am alerted if I hear my name. Then I say, 'That is an interesting
point. Could you repeat your question so I can consider my response
more thoughtfully?'" She seemed very proud of her strategy, although my

experience hearing people complain about needing to repeat questions during meetings suggests that some people may be on to her game.

Your ability to control your presence is limited in synchronous conversations. During the pandemic, when people were working from home and connecting to videoconferencing most of the day, many people reported how exhausted they felt. A videoconference meeting with a few people (maybe four or five) requires a focus that individuals are not used to. This intense environment where you can't look away can be draining. The larger meetings, especially those where everyone is not using their camera, or where it is impossible to see everyone on the monitor, provide opportunities for budgeted presence. In fact, when you are looking at the camera while on a call, your eyes can stray to a Google search bar without anyone knowing that you are checking your email.

Budgeted presence can mean that face-to-face, routine, weekly meetings can become somewhat tedious, with no one truly engaging in the meeting and repetition being a common remedy for people missing important material. To address this challenge, the members of one organization's executive team embraced the multicommunicating challenge while addressing the need for face-to-face interaction. They decided to allocate a certain part of each week where everyone was present in one conference room. They weren't having a meeting. They were just all available for potential face-to-face individual meetings, while they were also accomplishing tasks and engaged in other meetings and conversations using their digital devices. This allocated presence time was an interesting recognition of budgeted presence and the need to be available "visually and potentially" to each other but not necessarily through a traditional meeting format.

WHAT ARE THE TRADE-OFFS?

While budgeted presence can be very efficient, it can also be problematic. Communication is a human endeavor, so recognizing the human aspects of interaction are critical. Most of the drawbacks of budgeted presence are related to disrespecting your audience and missing critical information.

Disrespecting Your Audience

In addition to message or information loss due to budgeted presence, the possibility of hurting someone's feelings or appearing uncivil is high due to rapidly changing norms. Our society's rapid adoption of digital communication devices means that the norms for what is appropriate and what is not are constantly changing. My research into multicommunicating found that people often said that they wouldn't multicommunicate when they were with their boss because they saw it as a sign of disrespect.[11] However, other people suggested that they are showing their boss that they are working hard if they are checking their phone during a meeting. To the extent that your audience member is made to feel as if their message is an unnecessary expenditure, you are bound to face hurt feelings, frustration, a lack of self-disclosure, and irritation.[12]

It is important to recognize that sometimes what is *relevant to us* is not the most important assessment to make. The short-term efficiencies of a conversation enabled by budgeted social presence provided by a digital device may in the long term erode a relationship. All communication is not efficient and is not meant to be efficient. Some communicators take longer to make a point than others.

The disadvantages of budgeted social presence are often voiced most loudly by those on the receiving end of budgeted presence: "My team members never pay attention during my meetings." "My boss is always on his phone while I am presenting." These multicommunicating behaviors are often categorized as rude, socially inept, and offensive.[13] Communication is an incredibly human endeavor. When individuals feel ignored or dismissed, they may feel upset and less comfortable or motivated to share information.

In one of my interviews, the vice president of sales in a consumer products company talked about a person in her organization:

> Every time I go into meetings with her, she is on her phone. Everyone
> talks about her. I feel like she should realize that no one around her is on
> their phones. But I guess she is just so engrossed she can't stop herself.
> It's too bad because she is pretty smart and has some good ideas but she

usually isn't plugged into what is going on in the meeting so we don't hear them. She has lost a lot of credibility here.

In this way, engaging in budgeted presence can be costly for relationships. This is so true that a term has emerged to describe the act of being snubbed by a phone. *Phubbing*—an actual word added to the *Oxford English Dictionary*—describes the situation where a person is engaged in a conversation with someone else and that person looks at their phone. Not surprisingly, researchers have found connections between phubbing and relationship dissatisfaction,[14] and between phubbing and employee engagement.[15]

Missing Critical Information

Ironically, many of the times that you choose to engage in budgeted social presence involve an individual whom you don't like, with whom you don't agree, or whom you don't find relevant. And while your decision might be efficient, if you are not dependent on this person for any resource, this decision could be very detrimental if you are dependent on this person. One executive I talked with described a controversial meeting where participants started working on their iPads as the conversation became more challenging: "I felt like when some of the topics turn uncomfortable, people would start picking up their phones or their iPads and focus on those. They were disengaged and didn't want their fingerprints on something that they didn't agree with." When people are able to use devices to avoid challenging conversations in meetings, the potential for collaboration and consensus building in the meeting can be affected.

While sometimes you deliberately use mobile devices to avoid a challenging topic or conversation, other times you may unintentionally miss out on an important moment or conversation because you are connected to your mobile devices. This challenge has inspired discussion of the importance of mindfulness and recognizing the power of "the moment." Impromptu conversations or hallway chatter happens less frequently when the focus of all interaction is placed on planned conversations or managing an inbox of messages. This loss of impromptu or spontaneous conversation, which often can occur during physical presence, was intensely felt during the pandemic when many organizational meetings were relegated to scheduled, online conversations.

WHEN SHOULD YOU CHOOSE BUDGETED PRESENCE?

When should we engage in budgeted presence? We need to weigh the costs of our informational and relationship needs. Additionally, we need to calculate the relevance of the content and the visibility of the practice to the people with whom we are talking. When you are in a large meeting room and no one can see you engaged in budgeted presence, at least you don't have to worry about appearing rude or uncivil. You are able to manage your relationship costs through the invisibility of the practice. Unfortunately, people often think they are invisible when they are not. I find when I am speaking in a room of seventy people that I still have a good sense of who is with me and who is not. Generally, when I hear someone typing furiously during my presentation, I tend to assume that they are not with me and that they are talking with friends rather than taking notes.

For each type of presence, three types of factors need to be considered: contextual, message, and relationship. Specifically, where are you? Contextual factors refer to the norms, response expectations, visibility, and time constraints associated with a particular presence choice. Next, what are you talking about? Message factors refer to the content of the message as it relates to sensitivity, salience, complexity, and ambiguity. And finally, with whom are you talking? Relationship factors refer to value, status, and interdependence. Consider your decision to engage in budgeted social presence as it relates to these three factors.

Where Are You?

From a contextual standpoint, thinking about where you are trying to be present is important to consider. What are the norms of the situation? If everyone else is engaging in budgeted presence, it could be that this type of social presence is expected within the organization. During the pandemic, budgeted presence became almost expected since you couldn't see what other people on a video call were actually doing and they couldn't really see what you were doing. I worry about the impact of such a long period of time (well over a year in some organizations), where expectations for budgeted presence were so pervasive throughout the workweek.

Be aware that by engaging in budgeted presence, you are reinforcing the norm. If you have high status in a meeting, you could be sending the signal that people who are busy and important need to be engaging in budgeted presence, since that is what you are exhibiting from an authority standpoint. My colleague at Georgetown University, Bob Bies, often talks about how leaders are signal senders. If you are a leader and you are frustrated by your organization's overdependence on budgeted presence, be aware of the signal that you are sending. Similarly, if you are leader and have not been explicit about expectations regarding digital device use within meetings, you are giving up control of those norms to the people in your organization. It has been interesting to me that in many of my executive classes, participants will be frustrated by the way individuals are using communication devices in their organization but they also feel that they can't bring the subject up. One participant said, "I get so frustrated when I have someone in my office and they are checking messages while I am talking. It is so disrespectful. But I don't want to say anything because I will just come off as old and cranky."

It seems that there is a perception that the norms around digital device use are driven by different generations. However, digital device use has become so pervasive that it is hard to argue that one generation uses devices in a pattern significantly different from another generation. In fact, the applications are changing so fast that many seniors in college look at mobile device use differently than freshmen. Because of the rapidly changing nature of digital device use, being explicit about expectations is more important. This means explaining your approach to the use of digital devices to your team but also within the context of specific conversations. For example, as leader of a team, you might have a conversation about norms you are interested in developing surrounding digital devices. Or you might also explain to someone at the start of a conversation, "Our team is in the middle of a huge contract negotiation, so if someone calls me about that, I will have to answer." The expectation about what is appropriate and what is not changes rapidly and requires a conversation at all levels within an organization, team, or relationship.

What Are You Talking About?

Message factors also contribute to the selection of budgeted presence. If a message is extremely sensitive or difficult, choosing to engage in budgeted presence to communicate that message or to engage in budgeted presence while receiving that message could appear very insensitive. Similarly, when a message is very important, it requires focus from all communicators involved. Complexity and ambiguity also play an important role in the decision to engage in budgeted presence. Messages that are simple and clear—because they might refer to directions, or let someone know you are in a meeting—can be easily sent when in budgeted presence. In fact, many tools on our digital devices support budgeted presence in this situation by providing pre-made notifications that can be sent at the touch of a button without typing in all the letters. Similarly, autocomplete allows people to text more efficiently by supplying common words or phrases. These tools might make sense for routine messages. However, complex or ambiguous messages require focus from both communicators to engage in the conversation necessary to manage the complexity or ambiguity.

Additionally, time is an important characteristic that can influence how social presence is constructed within a specific environment. For example, budgeted presence may seem appropriate during a crisis situation, where everyone in the organization is expected to be available at all times. Similarly, if time is short and a decision needs to be made quickly, communicators must prioritize their presence decisions to meet the needs of their most important communicators.

With Whom Are You Talking?

Response expectations can also influence the context. If you are on an audio conference call and your audio is muted, no one on the call probably expects a quick response from you. If the meeting is set up so that people will be asked to contribute during specific times, then you know that you will not have the added pressure to respond. As a result, this context provides more freedom to engage in budgeted presence. In conversations where you are not visible, you have more flexibility to engage in budgeted presence. While you may believe that you can listen to the conversation while also texting a friend, the extent to which your audience knows that you are doing that may influence their perceptions of you and how you value their relationship.

Relationship factors are also connected to whom you are interacting with. Relationship factors refer to the impact of the act of multicommunicating or engaging in budgeted social presence on the relationship itself. If a relationship has high value or high status, engaging in budgeted presence might suggest that you don't value the relationship. In my research on multicommunicating, most people said that they often would multicommunicate except when it involved their boss.[16] They believed it was OK for their boss to multicommunicate when the boss was also talking to them but it was not OK for them to multicommunicate when the boss was trying to speak. Budgeted presence sends the signal that your audience is an expenditure of your presence, and when you engage in multiple conversations at once you may be suggesting that their presence is not worth your full attention. Finally, interdependence can have an impact on budgeted presence. The more interdependent you are on a specific audience for resources, the more likely you might be to engage in budgeted presence to reach that person or to avoid budgeted presence so as not to offend that person.

Should You Be Listening?

A final message consideration that also connects with the relationship factor is the perspective of your audience as opposed to your own. When your audience is talking about something that they feel is sensitive or important, they expect your focused attention, even if you don't see the topic as sensitive or important. If the relationship matters to you, then the perspective of that person on the topic being discussed is critical to consider. Most of the research exploring the intrusivity of the cellphone on conversations refers to those conversations that are sensitive or important.[17] Several interviewees talked about the challenge of conversations where they were talking about something important but their conversational partner was distracted by their phone. One said,

> Something happened at work where I was really upset. I felt like my boss wasn't listening to me and it made me feel like I wasn't respected. Well, I was telling my husband this story while I was making dinner and I looked up and he was answering his email. I couldn't believe it. I didn't even want to say anything because my whole conversation was about having someone not listening to me and here he was not listening to me. It was horrible.

Another person shared a work example: "I was talking to a client about a strategy and he heard me typing on my computer. He told me he would call back when he had my attention. I tried to tell him that I was typing notes but I don't think he believed me."

We often mistakenly think of communication as a way to transmit an idea from our head to someone else's head. Communication is much more than that. While we may believe we can manage multiple messages at once to different people, the people on the receiving end of our conversations often believe they need more of our focus. Viewing our conversational partners as messages to be juggled as efficiently as possible may often dismiss the relationship component of every interaction. Budgeted

---

TAKEAWAYS FROM CHAPTER 1

- Examine the relationship and task dimensions of your message.
- Develop strategic criteria for your conversations.
- Intentionally choose channels that support your needs.
- Create a more intentional approach to your conversations.
- Engage in conversations about your expectations about social presence.

presence is becoming almost a necessity, which is why it is critical to reflect on when, where, and with whom we engage in this type of presence. We can't always be intentional and proactive in the way we approach our mobile devices, but understanding the options available and reflecting on the implications of these options may help us begin to be more strategic about these choices.

REFLECTION

- When do you most often choose budgeted social presence?
- Are there certain people with whom you tend to choose to enact budgeted social presence?
- What are the primary drivers of your decision to engage in budgeted social presence?
- When has budgeted social presence been most successful for you?
- When has budgeted social presence created problems for you?
- How do you feel when someone chooses budgeted social presence with you?

EXERCISE

Choose a person who you tend to have challenging interactions with. Specifically, this is a situation where

- you do not see the issue the same way the other person does,
- you care about the issue—the stakes are high, and
- you are interdependent on this person—your success is interconnected with something that they are doing.

Now, when you engage in a conversation with this person, try turning off your phone or putting it in a place where you will not feel it vibrate and you will not see it. It could be synchronous (a face-to-face conversation, video or phone) or asynchronous (email or text). Try to have a conversation with this person about this issue without multicommunicating. In subsequent chapters, we will be talking about other types of presence choices. The main issue here is that you are *not* choosing budgeted presence. Have the conversation and then reflect. How did it go? Did you notice anything different?

This chapter has focused on the workplace environment. However, our workplace often merges with our home life. We absolutely saw this in an extreme way when the coronavirus created the need for home and work to collide. Our workplace merged into home and home into work. The next chapter focuses on budgeted presence within home and educational environments.

NOTES

1. Cameron Pierce and Greta Underhill, "Expectations of Technology Use during Meetings: An Experimental Test of Manager Policy, Device Use, and Task-Acknowledgement," *Mobile Media and Communication* 9, no. 1 (2020): 78–102, doi: 10.1177/2050157920927049.

2. Ryan J. Allred and John P. Crowley, "The "Mere Presence" Hypothesis: Investigating the Nonverbal Effects of Cell-Phone Presence on Conversation Satisfaction," *Communication Studies* 68, no. 1 (2017): 22–36, doi:10.1080/10510974.2016.1241292.

3. Ann Cameron, Jane Webster, Henri Barki, and Ana Ortiz de Guinea, "Four Common Multicommunicating Misconceptions," *European Journal of Information Systems* 25, no. 5 (2017): 465–71.

4. Bill Thornton, Alyson Faires, Maija Robbins, and Eric Rollins, "The Mere Presence of a Cell Phone May Be Distracting: Implications for Attention and Task Performance," *Social Psychology* 45, no. 6 (2014): 479–88, doi:10.1027/1864-9335/a000216.

5. Alice Marwick and danah boyd, "I Tweet Honestly, I Tweet Passionately: Twitter Users, Context Collapse, and the Imagined Audience," *New Media & Society* 13, no. 1 (2010): 114–33, doi:10.1177/1461444810365313.

6. James Roberts, Luc Yaya, and Chris Manolis, "The Invisible Addiction: Cell-Phone Activities and Addiction among Male and Female College Students," *Journal of Behavioral Addictions* 3, no. 4 (2014): 254–65, doi:10.1556/JBA.3.2014.015.

7. Rich Ling, *New Tech New Ties: How Mobile Communication Is Reshaping Social Cohesion* (Cambridge, MA: MIT Press, 2008).

8. Christian Licoppe, "Connected Presence: The Emergence of a New Repertoire for Managing Social Relationships in a Changing Communications Technoscape," *Environment and Planning: Society and Space* 22, no. 1 (2004): 135–56.

9. Leslie A. Perlow, *Sleeping with Your Smartphone: How to Break the 24/7 Habit and Change the Way You Work* (Boston: Harvard Business Review Press, 2012).

10. Keri Stephens, "Multiple Conversations during Organizational Meetings:

Development of the Multicommunicating Scale," *Management Communication Quarterly* 23, no. 1 (2012): 195–223.

11. Jeanine Warisse Turner and N. Lamar Reinsch, "Successful and Unsuccessful Multicommunication Episodes: Engaging in Dialogue or Juggling Messages?" *Information Systems Frontiers* 12, no. 3 (2010): 277–85, doi:10.1007/s10796-009 -9175-y.

12. Emily Paskewitzand Stephenson Beck, "Exploring Perceptions of Multicommunicator Texting during Meetings," *Computers in Human Behavior* 101 (2019): 238–47.

13. Peter Cardon and Ying Dai, "Mobile Phone Use in Meetings among Chinese Professionals: Perspectives on Multicommunicating and Civility," *Global Advances in Business Communication* 3, no. 1 (2014): article 2.

14. Varoth Chotpitayasunondh and M. Douglas Karen, "How 'Phubbing' Becomes the Norm: The Antecedents and Consequences of Snubbing via Smartphone," *Computers in Human Behavior* 63 (2016): 9–18.

15. James A. Roberts and Meredith E. David, "Put Down Your Phones and Listen to Me: How Boss Phubbing Undermines the Psychological Conditions Necessary for Employee Engagement," *Computers in Human Behavior* 75 (2017): 206–17.

16. Jeanine Warisse Turner and N. Lamar Reinsch Jr., "The Business Communicator as Presence Allocator: Multicommunicating, Equivocality, and Status at Work," *Journal of Business Communication* 44, no. 1 (2007): 36–58, doi:10.1177/00219 43606295779.

17. Andrew K. Przyblylski and Netta Weinstein, "Can You Connect with Me Now? How the Presence of Mobile Communication Technology Influences Face-to-Face Conversation Quality," *Journal of Social and Personal Relationships* 30, no. 3 (2013): 237–46, doi:10.1177/0265407512453827.

2

Budgeted Presence outside the Workplace

What does budgeted presence look like in your homes? In your schools? Digital devices have infiltrated every aspect of your lives. You sleep near your device. You are at dinner with your device. You are at the park with your device. You walk from room to room in your home with your device. You navigate work challenges while at home with your device. I regularly hear these complaints when I ask people about their digital devices: "My children are never paying attention to me." "Our dinners are miserable because their eyes are glued to their phone the whole time." "My students are not responsive in class." "My husband is always on his phone at dinner."

Around the globe, families and friends are negotiating digital devices as they encroach on our relationships and family life. This collision of work and home was exacerbated in March 2020 due to the COVID-19 pandemic, when most of the world's schools closed, affecting 90 percent of the world's students with little to no time for planning or reflection.[1] Parents were trying to work from home while also trying to manage their children's school day. Budgeted presence wasn't just a choice but a necessity.

But these challenges have been ongoing as mobile devices have diffused. In 2019, I visited with a religious sister in a community in Africa who was developing training programs for families to address the challenge of digital devices. A woman I taught in a leadership program in Qatar talked about how her children created a PowerPoint presentation to convince her that they needed access to a smartphone. The tech billionaire and cofounder of Microsoft Bill Gates argues that children should not get smartphones until they are fourteen years old.[2] Globally, children are increasingly given access to smartphones. A 2017 CNN report found that within the United States, about 45 percent of children receive access to a smartphone between the ages of ten and twelve.[3] Similar numbers were found for Europe and higher numbers in South Korea and South Africa. This research was focused on smartphones but did not address digital tablets and toys that start much earlier and introduce children to the idea of walking around with a technological device that distracts them from conversation. In fact, one woman in my executive education class told me about a friend of hers who taught third grade. In her classroom, she had a large transparent shoe organizer that she hung over the door. Each third grader would enter the classroom and put their phone in the organizer. When it was time to take attendance, the teacher glanced at the organizer to see which phones were missing. Only one little third-grade girl in the class did not have a mobile device, so the teacher had to physically look for her. For everyone else, she could just take attendance by looking at the phones.

Necessarily, because everyone has access to digital devices, budgeted presence makes up most of our social presence. It is your default state. You start in budgeted presence and then you make intentional decisions to move to another type of presence. Physical presence becomes background noise for your digital devices. Just as I mentioned when I discussed the work environment, the opportunity for impromptu conversations is diminished. Long, awkward pauses disappear as you can be quickly rescued from a difficult conversation with a text message or email you *need* to read.

This chapter explores changing norms for social presence outside the work environment and the implications of budgeted presence outside work with friendships, families, and educational environments.

HOW ARE CHANGING NORMS AFFECTING BUDGETED PRESENCE OUTSIDE WORK?

Norms are quickly evolving around multicommunicating as people decide whether it is acceptable or rude. This rapid evolution can be traced to the way the mobile device is taken for granted and has been seamlessly embedded within the fabric of our organizations and our communication use.[4] The absence of rules or norms results in people carrying the device around with them in a constant state of digital distraction.[5] More and more examples of people engaging in conversations while on their phone can be seen in commercials, television, movies, and books, illustrating the growing acceptance and diffusion of this behavior in every aspect of our lives. Additionally, apps like Snapchat and Instagram Stories that encourage daily interaction of some kind (usually the exchange of a photo) point to the importance placed on connecting in some small way to a specific group of people each day. People count how many days they have been able to keep a specific chat going, and the increasing number is a measure of intimacy or friendship. I talked with one person who traveled out of the country and gave his phone to a friend to maintain the "streak" so he wouldn't ruin his number. He had been sending a photo to this friend for over 450 days. This constant connection necessarily leads to budgeted presence. These changing norms, as well as the blurred line between work and home, have had a significant impact on the choice of budgeted presence at home.

Work Has Invaded Your Home

The growth of budgeted presence has also been fueled by the disappearance of the line between work and home. When you are faced with deadlines from work in your home environment that may not have any specific deadlines regarding interaction (I am not referring here to logistical deadlines involving transporting people from one activity to another), you often try to just "finish this one thing." Without clear guidelines from your boss for expectations for communication while at home, you may feel as if your home has become just another environment where work happens. As work infiltrates the home, family members continuously learn to accept the presence of work in their home life. One woman talked about her acceptance of her husband's budgeted presence because of his consulting career:

I try to be very respectful if it's like something that is work-related. Even if we're having dinner and someone calls him. At the beginning it was really, really bothering me. But then we have always been pretty supportive of each other's careers. So I have got to the point of like understanding that. But if it is something not work-related, then yes, I ask if he could just pay attention to whatever I'm saying because otherwise he's going to drive me crazy for me to repeat, "What did I say?"

HOW IS BUDGETED PRESENCE AFFECTING YOUR FRIENDSHIPS?

Most of my interviewees lament the frustration and disappointment of being with friends who are clearly not prioritizing their relationship by being on their mobile devices. Said one woman,

> I get so upset when I make plans to be with someone and it seems like they didn't make plans at all. They might be physically with me but they are really holding friend office hours with about ten other people. So I just sit there eating while they keep up with all of their friends. I have this one friend who always apologizes. And I think, what are you sorry about? Are you sorry you are talking to someone else while we are supposed to be having dinner or sorry that I don't have anyone else to talk to while we are supposed to be having dinner?

Budgeted presence has the most negative impact on friendships when one person is focused on their phone and the other person has decided not to. There are many examples of friends going out together where both friends step in and out of their physical conversation to connect with their friends on mobile devices. You often can see groups of friends sitting together at a Starbucks or hanging out at a park where everyone in the group is on their phones. When the decision is made either intentionally or unintentionally that everyone will be choosing budgeted presence, the choice is much less problematic.

While teaching a class of executives in Doha, one woman told me about her frustration about a recent conversation with a friend. The friend had invited her to get together, but when they met, her friend kept texting and checking her social media. When the woman asked her friend to stop using her phone and talk with her, the friend said, "I don't have anything to talk about." Conversation, and maintaining the rhythm of a conversation, has become even more of an art. The immediate feedback and instant connection of your mobile device is much easier to interact with than the sometimes-awkward experience of face-to-face conversations. Face-to-face conversation can seem like a fact-finding mission where each person is trying to discover an interesting shared experience or idea that will stimulate the interaction. This discovery can involve trial and error as each person asks questions or offers experiences until something takes hold that helps the conversation progress seem more effortless. Digital devices, in their ability to provide instant gratification when it comes to conversation through its variety of platform choices, has revealed the slow and sometimes cumbersome nature of face-to-face interactions.

Some researchers suggest that we are losing the ability to have conversations.[6] People describe a type of social autism. Autism describes a complex development disorder that neurologically affects the way an individual processes social cues. A person with autism may not see the same cues in a conversation that a neurotypical person may. This inability to pick up on certain social cues can make communication problematic. In a similar way, when you are choosing budgeted presence, you often miss cues because you are attempting to engage in multiple conversations at the same time. Necessary cues are missed. One woman talked with me about what she sees with her family as it relates to social cues:

> I can really see this generationally with my family. The people in my family that are younger just aren't able to read emotions the way that people that are older are. And it just is I think a byproduct of the fact that they don't have as much chance to do it. They're not forced to do it, right? So even interactions like going inside and ordering something at the McDonald's and not wanting to have to actually talk to the person behind the counter. It's fascinating, but my daughter hates doing it. She's like, "Why can't I just like order ahead?"

Ironically, you often choose budgeted presence when you are talking to someone you don't like or don't agree with, and these may be the people you should be focusing on the most. In my classes, when I talk about persuasion, I argue that when you do not agree with a person's perspective and you are trying to get them to change their mind about something, you need more data. You have a specific way of seeing the world and particular data in a context that you are attending to that leads you to your conclusion. When someone else is forming a different conclusion, necessarily she is paying attention to different data. The only way to find out what that person is paying attention to is to talk to her about her perspective. You need to engage her in a conversation to find out why she thinks the way that she does so you will be in a better position to understand her perspective and tailor a message for her. When you are engaged in budgeted presence and the other person sees that you are not giving her your undivided attention, she is less likely and is less motivated to share the information. As a result, you are not able to gain the knowledge necessary to create a more focused and targeted message for persuasion.

Another interviewee referred to the changing use of digital devices where people choose to broadcast messages rather than interact:

> She'll text. She's usually always on broadcast, right? So for Laureen, it's
> fascinating because technology gives her more ways to broadcast. So
> ever since I was young, I mean my, this is going to sound horrible, but
> I had a roommate Mary when I was younger and Mary can tell you that
> Laureen would call and I would put the phone on speaker and I would
> put the phone down and I would be doing my laundry and she's on
> broadcast. So now she has all these social media platforms—Facebook,
> Instagram, or texting individuals but still broadcast and everyone in her
> family does it. They are all always on broadcast.

HOW IS BUDGETED PRESENCE AFFECTING YOUR FAMILY TIME?

Families constitute a unique challenge for budgeted presence. Since budgeted presence is your default state, you may refer to your device even more while you are at home than you do at work. Families don't have the same missions, tasks, or critical meetings that might be in place at work. Dinner is one time when families traditionally gathered together, but dinner time is not as sacred as it once was, with increasing research pointing to the intrusion of smartphones into this space.[7] Opportunities for your family to gather to share their day requires intentional effort. As a result, the space inside the home can become a container for your family but not a place where the family works together toward anything. You could be sitting next to a family member as both of you engage in texting on your digital device. Any conversation that is started is often interrupted by someone's text or social media post. In this way, the family space becomes a giant waiting room for other big activities. And even big activities like birthday celebrations, or holidays like Thanksgiving in America, involve fewer conversations.

One of the most poignant vignettes I have seen that describes the implications of budgeted presence on families is a 2018 commercial for IKEA, the Swedish furniture company. In the commercial, families sit around tables and compete in a game show involving family knowledge. The announcer asks members of the family questions. If the person being quizzed gets the answer right, the person can remain at the table. However, if the person does not answer the question correctly, they must leave the table. In the commercial, the families are very good at answering the questions about celebrities, memes, or a new app. When the questions become more specific to family members—like "Where did your parents meet?" "What is your son's favorite book?" or "What is your wife's dream?"—the family members are stumped and are forced to leave the table. The commercial reveals the changing nature of conversation within families, where the sharing of information is stifled by the presence of digital devices. Historical information and family memories are lost, as the time for those conversations never comes up.

I have worked at Georgetown University for the last twenty-three years. During that time, I have had three children. I used to feel very guilty, and still do, about being away from my family as a working mom. I often tried to work from home on days when I wasn't teaching so I could spend more time with my children. I would worry about not being a mom who stayed home all the time, completely devoted to raising her family. However, in studying the developments of communication technology over time, I have seen the digital device to be a great equalizer between working and nonworking parents. When a child sees his mother on her digital device, he can't tell if she is accomplishing work or texting a friend. The distracted mom looks the same in both settings.

In about 2012, I was waiting in line with my twelve-year-old daughter for the It's a Small World ride at Disney World. It was pouring down rain. This was not our first rodeo at Disney World. However, in front of us were a man and a little girl. The little girl had never been to Disney World before and was very excited to be in line. She was bouncing with energy. Despite the rain and the forty-five-minute line, she was excited about the chance to go on the ride. She kept pulling on the man's leg and talking about the ride. Meanwhile, he was engaged in budgeted presence, checking his phone and responding intermittently to her questions. Finally, when it was time to get on the ride, they were in the boat directly in front of us. I assumed that once they were on the ride he would stop looking at his phone. But he didn't. I actually took a picture of them because I was appalled that he waited for forty-five minutes in the rain with a child who presumably meant something to him and he was missing the whole activity. He missed her excitement. He missed her wide-eyed amazement. He missed her laughter. I know what you are thinking. Why weren't you paying attention to your daughter instead of this other family while you were on the It's a Small World ride? Point taken! However, I found this example to be incredibly poignant. When we pride ourselves on our ability to engage in multiple conversations at once and pat ourselves on the back for availability and responsiveness, what might be the costs to the relationships around us?

In Doha, we also talked about the way digital devices are encroaching on family conversations. One woman talked about the Majlis. The Majlis is an integral part of Qatari culture and describes "place of seating." The Majlis is often a room where "male family members gather to discuss serious matters such as marriages, traveling, financial status, political situations, and future challenges."[8] In a culture that values family gather-ings and interaction, she commented on how phones and iPads were be-coming a huge distraction to communication. It used to be that children would learn the norms and protocols of the Majlis—who to greet first, how to greet, how to pour tea—from watching others and being socialized within that community. "Now we have classes for children to teach them what to do." Gaming systems and technology have infiltrated the Majlis, changing the nature of the social presence inside. People still convene in the Majlis, but the nature of the interaction has changed.

One of the challenging aspects of budgeted presence in the family is the way you are often unaware of how disengaged you are with the people around you. I think it goes back to the fact that humans can't cognitively multitask. And multicommunication is much more cognitively complex than multitasking because you are managing multiple roles and expec-tations as you move from one conversation to another. Some communi-cation researchers argue that you cannot not communicate.[9] What they mean by this is that you are always communicating through your verbal and nonverbal behavior. When you are walking into a room texting, you are communicating with others in the room that you are not available. The likelihood that someone will interrupt you from your device and strike up a conversation with you is much lower than if you just walked into the room without the phone. In 2017, I was talking to an executive who told me the story of how her phone use had crept into her family time without her realizing it. She works for a large nonprofit organization where employees are given the opportunity, after being at the company for a certain number of years, to take time off from work for six weeks and engage in some activity that is not work related. The time off is called "renewal." The concept reminds me somewhat of a sabbatical. The idea is that employees will step out of the workplace and come back more energized. "This happened about ten years ago, and the company had just given me a phone." She didn't realize how attached she had become to the phone. She had also just had the opportunity to come up for her "renewal" so the family was going to take a month off to go on vacation:

I remember the reaction of my 11-year-old son when I told him that I would not be allowed to take my phone with me on vacation because I was supposed to be detached from work. He said "That's the best thing I have ever heard." It really struck me and as I think back now, I probably was really attached to my phone. And because it was so long ago at a time when they didn't have phones, my phone use was even more pronounced. My children didn't have phones so they could really see my attachment.

Another woman similarly shared her frustration with her own smartphone use. "Yesterday I was playing with my two-year old son. I needed to check some messages on my phone during the game. At one point, my son became so frustrated that he grabbed the phone and threw it across the room." This example so poignantly reflects the insidious nature of phone use. A game that a two-year-old plays is probably not that complex. So it is actually cognitively possible for this mother to check her messages and still "play" the game. But the relational impact is much different. The challenge with budgeted presence can often appear in the delicate balance between weighing the needs of specific tasks and the relationship needs of the other conversations in which you are participating.

HOW IS BUDGETED PRESENCE AFFECTING THE CLASSROOM?

The introduction of communication devices into the classroom has influenced the behavior of faculty, the behavior of the students, and the overall culture of the classroom. When a student had nothing else to do but doodle on their paper, they often would decide to just give in to the experience and listen to the lecture. In fact, the students have been learning about how to pretend to pay attention throughout their school experience. So by the time students enter the university, especially at a competitive school like Georgetown, they have mastered the art of pretending to pay attention in class. However, once students had laptops with digital connectivity in front of them, the fabric of the classroom changed. Faculty could see that students were not paying attention, and they didn't know what to do about it. When you face an audience engaged in budgeted presence, you visibly see that "they are just not that into you."

This lack of attention can be crushing to a teacher but is also challenging for students. During COVID-19, in June 2020, my colleagues and I conducted a study to examine the impact of the suddenly online environment on the graduate student experience.[10] The distractions around them were debilitating to many students. Said one student,

> I am living with my grandmother here who's like paralyzed and she
> has special needs and normally we have people who come in part-time
> who help out with her but that's not happening because we're all under
> lockdown so things are a little bit more stressful and I don't know it just
> doesn't feel normal. The distractions make it impossible for me to focus.
> I try to make it as normal as possible by focusing on the screen but my
> email and messages are all right there on the same screen.

Said another student, "I share the same room with my boyfriend. So I don't have an independent space. Whenever I have class, my boyfriend is next to me, having meetings, or talking. Sometimes he just passes by behind me. Basically, my boyfriend is in my class. It is really hard to focus."

Impact on Faculty

This lack of engagement has an immediate impact on the faculty. Just as I discussed in the work-related section, presenting to a room of people who are not paying attention can take energy and motivation away from the presenter. I regularly conduct an exercise in class where I ask people to pair up. I ask one person in each pair to be a talker and the other to be a listener. I then ask the talker to talk for two minutes. During the first minute, the listener should pay close attention and be a great listener. During the second minute, the listener should not pay attention at all, should attempt to be a bad listener, and is free to look at their phones or employ other distractions.

This exercise is a real revelation to the talkers. Even though they all heard the instructions at the same time and knew that their listener was "pretending" during both minutes, the actions of the listener still make a huge impact on the ability of the talker to talk. When the talker has the listener's attention, she is articulate, talks with few vocal segregates (uh, um, ah, you know), and feels energized by the interaction. When the talker loses the listener's attention, she feels disconnected, and her argument becomes disjointed. She has more vocal segregates and has a hard time remembering her train of thought. Said one participant, "During the first minute I was so smooth! But during the second minute I kept forgetting what I was saying." The room usually gets louder as talkers try to get the listeners' attention through sound. This exercise shows the dynamic and reciprocal nature of communication and conversation. When you know that your audience is not listening or not engaged, you are not as effective as a communicator.

A number of faculty with whom I have talked have decided to retire early. With the tenure process in many universities, faculty usually have the choice of when to retire. However, the last ten years has changed the nature of interaction within the classroom. Said one faculty member who taught communication, "It's just not fun anymore. I feel like I need to be entertaining all the time. I am not a comedian or a performer. I went into teaching because I loved the discussion around ideas and the learning that took place in the classroom. Now it seems like the students are always disappointed. You just can't compete with a smartphone. I guess it is time for me to stop."

Impact on Students

I remember a time when I would enter a classroom at the beginning of class and I needed to tell everyone to settle down because everyone was talking and I needed them to begin to focus on the class. But now the room is quiet. Everyone is on their laptops or phones, talking with someone else or checking social media but not talking with anyone who is physically present. I think I noticed this change the most when I taught a class in a building at Georgetown called Walsh in 2007. Walsh is an older building that is a few blocks off of campus and sometimes had problems with its wireless connection. The students were really loud that morning. It was the first day of class, and I remembered being surprised to hear such a talkative room. The comparison with my other classes called attention to it for me. So I commented on how friendly everyone was. One student offered, "We can't get to the internet so there is nothing else to do." This comment struck me and reinforced how ubiquitous devices were changing the nature of the student experience. The subtle change of the start of class escaped my notice until I saw the stark difference between this class and my other classes.

In about 2007, I started to see campaigns within universities where students were asked to give up their technology for periods to see the impact this would have on their life. Jennifer Woolard is a psychology professor at Georgetown, and she taught a course where part of it involved reflecting on the impact of communication devices on everyday life. I had the opportunity to do focus groups with her students. One student talked about how hard it was to be a freshman and meet people: "You actually don't have to make new friends because you can bring all of your high school friends to school with you. There is really only about a three-week window when it is acceptable to introduce yourself to another person and say where you are from. After that, it is rude to interrupt someone at the beginning of class when they are on their technology to talk. When everyone is walking around with their phone, how can you ever break in? It's just too hard."

A number of challenges have been found with multicommunicating by students in the classroom environment. Research has found significant drops in grades associated with in-class phone use.[11] Similarly, students who report multicommunicating behaviors also report lower grade point averages.[12] Faculty report decreases in exam performance and long-term retention of material as a result of digital devices in class.[13] And unfortunately, the problems with the use of digital devices in class is not limited to its impact on the user. Studies have found that students who can see another student using a laptop score lower on tests of performance than those who cannot.[14] In fact, the student sitting behind and observing someone on their laptop is actually more distracted than the laptop user because the observer has no control over the laptop and so is continuously distracted by the changing images.

WHEN SHOULD YOU CHOOSE BUDGETED PRESENCE?

The criteria you use to govern choice of budgeted presence within these contexts are similar to those that you use for business settings. You need to consider the informational and relational costs of allocating only part of your attention to the people with whom you are communicating. You also need to calculate the relevance of the content and the visibility of the practice vis-à-vis other interaction partners. What is different about our relationships outside a business context is that we sometimes weigh informational costs more heavily, while your home or friendships may weigh more heavily from a relationship standpoint. Budgeted presence necessarily means you are multicommunicating, which means you are trying to engage in multiple conversations at once. I am not talking about times when you are at home alone checking your work email. Your lack of boundaries between work and home is not a social presence problem. I am only talking about times when you are choosing budgeted presence.

Where Are You?

Consider your visibility. Parents often complain because their children are always on their devices, but then they are also not monitoring their own use of these devices. Digital devices diffused so quickly that there has not been time for people to realize the impact of these devices on lives and relationships. We have a huge population of parents who did not grow up with a digital device and have had to figure it out as they watch their children grow up with them. Because digital devices are your default choice or the choice you are primarily in while you are at rest, you must be very intentional about the places where you will engage with it and the places where you won't. The first step might be to examine parts of your life and to decide when you would like to be open to conversation. Are there certain times that you would like to be sacred? Many people talk about how their families never got up from the table to answer the phone when they were growing up. The difference now is that you are managing not one device that is hanging on the wall across the room or in the next room but as many devices as there are people at the dinner table. And each one of these people has a network of people to whom they have access or have responsibilities to which they feel obligated that might interfere with your sense of what constitutes "family time." This decision may not be just an individual decision but may also need to include a conversation with all family members.

Similarly, when you are with your friends, you might make a conscious decision about the type of interaction you would like to have with your friends. Know that choosing budgeted presence might be efficient for you but could limit the depth of conversation that you will have during your time with your friend.

What Are You Talking About?

Another challenge with digital devices is an intentional requirement to consider your audience and not yourself. When you choose budgeted presence, it is usually about you and not about the people that you are with. Some people have asked if budgeted presence is only a problem in face-to-face communication where people can see you. I would argue it is easiest to choose budgeted presence when people can't see you, but you still will not be able to concentrate on what the other communicators are saying if you are engaging in multiple conversations. As mentioned above, all the research on multitasking says that humans actually cannot do it. You might think that younger generations are better at multitasking. Their minds are no different in their ability to do two things at once—they can't. However, the younger generation, because they have grown up multitasking, definitely feel more comfortable doing it.

If you are meeting with someone and talking about something that is not very serious (and when I say serious, I mean serious to the other person and not just serious to you), it is important to remember that choosing budgeted presence will signal that you are not as committed to the conversation.

With Whom Are You Talking?

Relationship factors can be the best way to make a decision about whether to choose budgeted presence. In this case, you need to think of life as a marathon and not a sprint. Budgeted presence will always be the most efficient and allow you to get many things done at once. Often with your family, when there is no specific activity on the agenda or task that everyone is working toward, the phone becomes an easy way to manage the information overload that is overwhelming us on a daily basis. But a short-term decision to choose budgeted presence can influence the development of your relationships over time. One woman talked about this challenge: "I have found that we don't know each other as well anymore and we actually have less to talk about. It is kind of funny that conversation can lead to more conversation. I used to talk everyday with my husband about what was going on at work. Now because of our devices in the house, it seems like we actually have less to talk about because I haven't kept him up to speed on things that are going on. Then it just becomes too much work to bring him up to speed. So we both say, 'How was your day?' and respond quickly, and go back to our phones."

Information overload is not just an adult problem. Some teenagers find that one of the biggest insults you can give to another person is leaving a text message on "read" for a long period of time without responding. Or alternatively, a child may post a picture that she has spent hours working on with filters and concentrating on composing just the right message to go with it. She sends it to her group of friends and waits anxiously for someone to respond with a like or an emoji. Another teenager talked with me about her need to respond with *something*, when someone texts her or sends her a message on a social media platform. This something could be a picture of the ceiling, or a picture with only a small piece of her face in it, but it is still a response. You might discount this kind of information overload as not important, but these decisions are critical to maintaining her social capital. Budgeted presence constitutes a large part of our family and friendship experiences. The intentional way we choose to be present is critical as we build our relationships.

TAKEAWAYS FROM CHAPTER 2

- Examine the relationship and task dimensions of your message.
- Develop strategic criteria for your conversations.
- Intentionally choose channels that support your needs.
- Create a more intentional approach to your conversations.

REFLECTION

- When do you most often choose budgeted social presence outside work?
- Are there certain people with whom you tend to choose budgeted social presence?
- What are the primary drivers of your decision to choose budgeted social presence?
- When has budgeted social presence been most successful for you outside work?
- When has budgeted social presence created problems for you outside work?
- How do you feel when someone chooses budgeted social presence with you?

EXERCISE

Choose a context outside work that really matters to you. Take one 3-hour period—it could be in the evening, the morning, over the weekend—and monitor how you and the people around you are using phones. Think of this as a mini-participant-observation study. Be a scientist. Keep track of the number of conversations, the type of conversations, and the impact of the digital devices in the room on those devices. We will continue to talk about ways to examine our use of digital devices in the next chapters. At this point, it is important to begin to be aware and cognizant of the impact of devices so you can then think about ways to address them. If you don't see the problem, it is hard to see a solution.

NOTES

1. Rebecca Winthrop, "Top 10 Risks and Opportunities for Education in the Face of COVID-19," Brookings: Education Plus Development, April 10, 2020, www.brookings.edu/blog/education-plus-development/2020/04/10/top-10-risks-and-opportunities-for-education-in-the-face-of-covid-19/.

2. Melanie Curtain, "Bill Gates Says This Is the 'Safest' Age to Give a Child a Smartphone," *Inc.*, May 10, 2017, www.inc.com/melanie-curtin/bill-gates-says-this-is-the-safest-age-to-give-a-child-a-smartphone.html.

3. Jacqueline Howard, "When Kids Get Their First Cell Phone around the World," CNN, December 11, 2017, www.cnn.com/2017/12/11/health/cell-phones-for-kids-parenting-without-borders-explainer-intl/index.html.

4. Richard Ling, *Taken for Grantedness: The Embedding of Mobile Communication into Society* (Cambridge, MA: MIT Press, 2012).

5. Keri Stephens, *Negotiating Control: Organizations and Mobile Communication* (New York: Oxford University Press, 2018).

6. Sherry Turkle, *Reclaiming Conversation: The Power of Talk in the Digital Age* (New York: Penguin, 2016).

7. Ryan J. Dwyer, Kostadin Kushlev, and Elizabeth W. Dunn, "Smartphone Use Undermines Enjoyment of Face-to-Face Social Interactions," *Journal of Experimental Social Psychology* 78 (2018): 238–39.

8. Fatma Salem, "Majlis Is a Key Feature of Civilisation in UAE," *Gulf News*, May 22, 2009, www.embracedoha.net/what-is-a-majlis/.

9. Paul Watzlawick, Janet Beavin Bavelas, and Don D. Jackson, *Pragmatics of Human Communication: A Study of Interactional Patterns, Pathologies, and Paradoxes* (New York: W. W. Norton, 1967).

10. Jeanine W. Turner, Fan Wang, and N. Lamar Reinsch, How to Be Socially Present When the Class Becomes 'Suddenly Distant,'" *Journal of Literacy and Technology: Special Issue for Suddenly Online – Considerations of Theory, Research, and Practice* 21, no. 2 (2020): 76–101.

11. Douglas Duncan, Angel Hoeskstra, and Wilcox Bethany, "Digital Devices, Distraction, and Student Performance: Does in-Class Cell Phone Use Reduce Learning?" *Astronomy Education* 11 (2012), doi:10.3847/AER2012011.

12. Lydia J. Burak, "Multitasking in the University Classroom," *International Journal for the Scholarship of Teaching & Learning* 6, no. 2 (2012): article 8, doi:10.2042 9/ijsotl.2012.060208.

13. Arnold Glass and Mengxue Kang," Dividing Attention in the Classroom Reduces Exam Performance," *Educational Psychology* 39, no. 3 (2019): 395–408, doi :10.1080/01443410.2018.1489046.

14. Faria Sana, Tina Weston, and Nicholas J. Cepeda, "Laptop Multitasking Hinders Classroom Learning for Both Users and Nearby Peers," *Computers & Education* 62 (2013): 24–31, doi:10.1016/j.compedu.2012.10.003.

Part II

"Turn Off Your Phone and Listen to Me"
Entitled Presence

You have probably used this phrase: "Turn off your phone and listen to me." Everyone around you is carrying a device that reminds you that the attention of your audience is never guaranteed. In this part, you'll learn about the costs and benefits of this choice.

3

Entitled Presence in the Workplace

Have you ever told someone to put their phone away and listen to you? If you have, then you know what it means to choose entitled presence. Entitled presence often comes when you are frustrated that someone is not listening or worried that they won't listen. When you choose entitled presence, you ask your audience to put their phones or digital devices away and concentrate on your message alone. Entitled presence can take place with just one other person, with a small group, or with a large audience.

WHAT IS ENTITLED PRESENCE?

Entitled presence privileges your message over all other messages that your audience might be receiving. The word "entitled" might seem a little negative—but it isn't meant to be. The word "entitled" is merely emphasizing the perspective behind the action. You think your message is more important than the other messages that your audience is receiving. You believe you are entitled to your audience's attention. The reason for the title of this type of presence is for you to take the time to consider what makes your message more special than any other so your audience should remove all distractions. It could be critical to the audience. So I am not saying that it is the wrong choice; I am just saying it is coming with a very strong expectation and assumption about the needs of your audience.

The use of mobile devices has spread throughout organizations. When you are facing a room full of smartphones, the knee-jerk reaction is often to just take the technology away. Many executives talk about how they have a box or basket in a meeting room. As people come in for the meeting, they tell them to deposit their digital device into the box until after the meeting. Similarly, some business people have expressed frustration when trying to have a conversation with another person and being continuously interrupted by their digital device. One human resource manager talked to me about her frustration when interviewees checked their phone for messages during a job interview with her.

Many managers whom I have interviewed refer to entitled presence as "old school." They suggest that taking technology away from people is generational. Said one manager,

> I'm old school enough for that—I get pissed when everybody's on their phone during the presentations or are looking up their stuff while we're trying to have a conversation. But when I pay for training, when I bring in consultants to explain the use of financial software or a technology to train up my staff or others—and that could be 10, 20 grand a clip, I don't want people on the phone with their boyfriend—I'm not paying for that. So it's kind of—I think I have occasionally done the, "Leave your thing in the box at the front of the room."

All these examples describe situations where communicators are choosing entitled social presence. In order to remove the competition created by the digital device, a communicator uses her own status or power to ensure that her own message is given priority by controlling her audience's access to competing messages that they might receive on their digital device. While entitled presence often involves control over access to technology, entitled presence is really about the control of attention. You can ask a person to look at you, or pay attention to you, even when a digital device is not available. Entitled presence is really about the control of the message environment, so audience members cannot receive messages other than the one the communicator is sending.

While people have been choosing entitled presence for centuries, the presence of digital devices has made the need more obvious. The cues that people were not listening used to be more subtle—someone writing a message on a notepad, someone doodling on a paper, someone looking in the distance. All these signals could also have meant that your audience

Review of Entitled Presence

Type of Presence	View of Audience	Goal	Benefits	Costs
Entitled	Container	Make audience listen and attend to your message	Remove technological distractions	Potential loss of your own credibility as a speaker

was engaged in your message and either taking notes or thoughtfully exploring your ideas in their mind. Now you are watching a sea of heads looking at their digital devices and not even pretending to smile at your jokes. The digital devices are clear reminders that your audience does not care. You may have the sense that your message is critical. However, everybody thinks the same thing about their own messages. Even though physical presence used to mean your audiences were somewhat captive in the same room, it never meant they were listening. The difference now is that you can see the digital devices that are pulling audiences away from your message.

So your answer is: *remove all distractions*! Then people will pay attention to you. But will they? Unfortunately, you can never *guarantee* an audience's attention. However, you can frustrate your audience by taking their technology away.

I was giving a seminar on presence to a group of women leaders at Georgetown University several years ago. We had a lively discussion, and afterward, one woman came up to ask additional questions. She specifically was interested in understanding "exiled presence." Since I had not used the word "exiled," I asked her to elaborate. "You know—exiled—when you take the technology away." While I have called that type of presence entitled, in reference to how the speaker views their message over the potential needs of the audience, her use of "exiled" is insightful. A person definitely could feel exiled if their technology is taken away. So removing technology could upset your audience. Although it may be tempting to remove distractions, the cost to your message or relationship may be too high.

The risk tends to come in the loss of social capital with your audience. They are used to using their digital devices, and they are juggling expectations from many of their own audiences. So who are you to take their digital device away? Most people whom I have interviewed and talked with describe entitled presence in frustrating terms. Executives lament when they are asked to put their phones away during a presentation or meeting. One communication director of an international organization was asked, along with her colleagues, to put her phone away at the beginning of a meeting: "I was blown away. I am supposed to be keeping up with what is going on globally across our organizations. How can I be expected to do that if my phone is not turned on?"

With COVID-19 and the immediate, global move from traditional physical office spaces to online virtual spaces, executives everywhere were faced with the need to communicate using video. While video communication has gradually become a tool used by most but not all the time, it became a tool used by all, almost all the time. The phrase "Zoom fatigue" entered the lexicon of most organizations. And the inability to guarantee entitled presence became more and more obvious. For you to tell people to put their technology away when you have no way of policing it seemed almost comical. Even status or visibility was not enough to help you guarantee attention in the same way you could if you asked people to put mobile devices away when physically present. The new work environment, necessary because of COVID-19, revealed how little control you actually have over your virtual audiences.

An interesting by-product of the pandemic with the constant use of video within organizations was the need for entitled presence to tell individuals to turn their cameras on. Audiences have the choice of turning on or off their camera. When an individual's camera is not on, their name or picture appears instead. When everyone chooses to turn off their camera, the call becomes a de facto audio call.

However, this situation is nothing like an audio call. When you are speaking on an audio call, you often assume people are halfway listening or multitasking, but you are not offended or troubled because the technology does not allow anyone to be seen. When speaking to a computer monitor filled with people who have chosen to turn off their cameras, their very choice not to show themselves when they actually could changes the dynamic of the situation. For me, this situation often made me feel more alone or maybe more desperate to get people to listen—almost like talking to a room where you see that no one is paying attention.

A norm began to emerge: you didn't tell people to turn off their technology, because it would effectively end the meeting, but told people to turn their cameras on. While this is not what you might traditionally think of as entitled presence, since most examples have involved removing access to other messages, telling people to turn their cameras on is a form of entitled presence because you are trying to control access to other messages and the way your audience is listening to you. As technologies and communication platforms evolve, forms of entitled presence may change, but the goal of entitled presence—control over your audience's attention—will stay the same.

WHAT TYPES OF ENTITLED PRESENCE ARE THERE?

Entitled presence can involve individual, organizational, or infrastructural imposed restrictions. We have talked about *individual* decisions, where a manager or a peer asks another person or group to put their technology away. However, choosing entitled presence is not limited to individuals. While you might feel frustrated or anxious about making the individual decision of having to tell someone to put their technology away, there are many times when the *organization* or the *infrastructure* supports you.

Organizational entitled presence involves situations where an organization imposes a rule about phone use. Some of these rules can be a little paradoxical. For example, one banking institution included in its employee handbook rules for mobile device use. Specifically, it suggested that employees were not supposed to check mobile devices during a presentation or meeting. Unfortunately, within the same handbook, it also emphasized the importance of responsiveness. It said that employees were expected to respond to messages from their supervisor within a 15-minute window. Ironically, these regulations could be very contradictory if meetings or presentations last longer than 15 minutes!

I learned about an interesting example of organizational entitled presence when I was teaching in an Executive Master's in Leadership program in Doha. This example was not about focusing on the organization, but rather keeping the organization from invading the home lives of employees. One of the executives shared with me an Instagram post by Her Royal Highness Sheikha Hind bint Hamad Al-Thani that addressed the intrusion of work into family conversations. While she was not trying to keep people from looking at their messages during work, she did try to keep people from looking at work messages while at home. She posted an email she had sent out as CEO of the Qatar Foundation saying "Hello, I'll be checking my email Sunday morning. I'm spending time with my family, hope you get to spend time with yours. Have a good weekend!" (Friday and Saturday constitutes the weekend in Doha.) Another chief operating officer of a banking organization told me about his chief financial officer's strict rule forbidding employees to check work-related communication after 5 pm on weekends.

Organizations can also create social norms for not communicating during a meeting. One individual that I talked with who worked for an association said she thought the culture of the national office was different from the regional or state offices: "We have a culture here—I often feel like people in the national office are on their phones more than when I'm with the states. Maybe it's because it's smaller groups." Another individual talked about the way a group can set a tone for acceptable use of mobile devices: "I think there is a lot of mirroring that happens. Like I feel like whoever sets the precedent in the room, like it is kind of followed."

Infrastructurally imposed entitled presence exists in many environments where the technology is not turned off by a single person or organization but by the building or wireless access. For example, some secure government buildings create special firewalls that prohibit individuals from receiving signals while in the building. To the extent that the audience has bought in to the need to be a part of that organization or environment, they participate by not bringing or using their digital device. Some protocols require employees to leave their devices in their car. Said one employee of the US Central Intelligence Agency (CIA), "Our meetings are very focused because no one has a phone. I mean, if someone were to come in and try to grab someone it would have to be in person, like Holly come in and say, 'You have a phone call,' or someone came in, 'Next meeting, team,' or something. But there's no electronic interaction."

Another infrastructure decision has been made by celebrities in the entertainment industry. While they can't control the venue, they have found ways to control mobile devices. Musicians like Alicia Keys, Steven Tyler, and Guns N' Roses and the comedian Dave Chappelle are a few entertainers who are trying to control technology use at their concerts. Bob Dylan, during a performance in Vienna in 2019, paused during his performance of "Blowin' in the Wind" to remind fans of his "no photos" policy.[1] In addition to the problem of concertgoers filming concerts and posting them online, entertainers argue that the distracted audience makes it harder for them to perform. For example, a technological system called Yondr provides a small pouch with a lock on it that concertgoers are given.[2] The audience can keep the phone with them but they cannot access the phone without leaving the concert hall and having the phone unlocked with a special key. The entertainer Kate Bush described it this way on her website, "I very much want to have contact with you as an audience, not with iPhones, iPads, or cameras. I know it's a lot to ask but it would allow us to all share in the experience together."[3]

WHO IS YOUR AUDIENCE?

During entitled presence, the communicator conceives of the audience as a container to be filled with messages or information. The audience could also be conceived of as a bank that is waiting for a deposit. You as the communicator believe you have information that the audience needs and you are making the decision for them that they must listen or attend to you. This commanding approach to presence can be offensive to an audience member who has had their agency or choice taken away from them. In addition, because of our overnetworked environment, the expectation that people can be reached has rearranged the potential priorities that people might have in physical spaces. Therefore, it is difficult to assess whether your audience truly needs the information that you are providing at that moment in time more than another message that is coming in.

In addition to commanding the attention of your audience, you are also commanding the specific type of attention that you want. For example, you are preventing your audience from taking notes on their mobile device if you take it away. One manager I talked with at a financial firm who was trying to generate conversation asked people to put their devices away. She said, "I felt that the meeting was about dialogue and collaboration. There was a person on his computer taking notes on everything we were saying. I said, 'Put it [the phone] away. This isn't a meeting to document what we are talking about. It is more of a brainstorming session.' He was not happy. But you can't brainstorm if you are recording notes. I need him to be future thinking, not past thinking."

Should the Choice Be Yours?

Digital devices have given people ubiquitous access, and when you take away that access, you create a complicated contract with your audience. This contract puts you in a higher power position with great expectations from your audience over how you use that time and attention. However, the very act of taking an audience's technology away sends a message that your own view is privileged over that of the audience, so it becomes difficult to simultaneously be audience-centered. It is hard to say, "Put away your technology" and then "I care about you and what you think."

WHERE'S THE CONTROL?

The focus of control with entitled presence is on the message. You want to control the information that is available at any one time to your audience, and you do this by removing access to other messages. A part of you might actually believe that by removing these technological distractions, the audience will have nothing left to do but focus on your message. If they could just put it away, they would realize how amazing and helpful my message can be for them.

The frustration I hear from presenters or conveners of meetings is palpable as they look out at the participants in their meetings with their heads buried in their digital devices. One of my interviews with an executive at a nonprofit talked about how he feels disrespected: "I think you are less enthused to work with someone when they are not giving you their full attention. And I think it's disrespectful. But that's on them, not on the speaker. I think there is more to be done in terms of creating self-awareness about the implications of having your head down and trying to do something in a conversation or meeting."

The *Wall Street Journal* ran a story that featured Jason Brown, the CEO of Brown, Parker & DeMarinis Advertising. "I lost it," says Brown. In his anger, he issued a companywide edict: "Don't show up at a meeting with me with your phone. If someone shows up with their phone, it'll be their last meeting."[4] In the same article, another CEO, Mat Shbia of United Wholesale Mortgage, not only banned cell phone use in meetings but also banned it from when employees are walking to and from meetings so as to encourage socialization. What is particularly interesting about the story of these CEOs is the status they were able to employ to underline the importance of the rule, and these executives still received pushback from disgruntled employees. Imagine how hard it is for a lower-level manager or peer to ask colleagues to put their devices away to focus on the meeting. This directive becomes even more difficult with people who are wearing smart devices. It is difficult to ask people to take off their watch or their glasses.

Within organizations, individuals are often a part of matrix organizations where individuals report to various teams and supervisors across the organization. This creates webs of complex relationships and responsibilities that make it difficult for any one person to manage another person's schedule. Because of the blurred lines between work life and personal life, there is an expectation that people are "reachable." This expectation contributes to anxiety when a person is suddenly disconnected. One person who I talked with discussed her anxiety this way: "At a meeting last week, someone asked the group to turn off their cell phones. I immediately felt uncomfortable and worried about what I am missing while I am 'disconnected.' I am unsure if I am able to focus clearly because I am more concerned with what emergency I am missing, whether it is work-related or personal."

While choosing entitled presence may seem like a logical and useful way to control the attention of your audience, the experience of the COVID-19 pandemic, when organizations were forced to move online quickly, revealed how little control communicators actually have. Audiences could turn off their cameras, transforming a synchronous videoconference into a podcast. Very quickly, it becomes difficult to visually monitor the people on your screen. The very camera that a person looks at to appear to be paying attention in the videoconference is located on the same desktop that is also serving up emails, social media updates, and shopping options.

WHAT ARE THE TRADE-OFFS?

Costs of entitled presence include your potential loss of credibility and social capital. The audience has no other message options now but you, so you'd better be relevant. I have taught executives how to conduct presentations for twenty years. I used to tell people to be dynamic and charismatic. But I don't tell them that anymore. I tell people to be *relevant*. I have talked with many managers who confidently argue the importance of removing technology from meetings to get attention. But I have also talked with just as many people who have been frustrated because they had their technology taken away. They are "exiled" from their network. They are captured rather than captivated. By removing their options, you have dramatically raised the stakes regarding expectations for your message. All focus is now on you and your message and a constant weighing of how your message measures up to the inconvenience and challenges associated with not being able to receive other messages. Said one executive about entitled presence, "People use technology differently, but to tell people they shouldn't, they should part with it is probably a conversation stopper. You probably have alienated a third of the room because people are just mad that you said that. You know what I mean? And now, I got a day-long retreat. What am I going to do with the anger?"

What Are the Benefits?

The advantages of entitled presence is the potential control of distractions. As speakers, we no longer need to compete with a YouTube video, a colleague's text, a tweet, or a Cyber Monday sale. We have the floor. But just having the floor does not guarantee attention or interaction. And possibly, the distraction of not having access to technology can overwhelm the audience and impede the opportunity for enthusiastic engagement.

The best way to get entitled presence is when your audience is desperate for your information. Be careful how you read this. They are desperate for your information, *not* you are desperate for them to have your information. There is a huge difference! But if they are so interested in your message, should you need to tell them to stop looking at their devices?

Organizationally imposed entitled presence or infrastructurally imposed presence might be easier because the fault or the anger doesn't come back on you. You can benefit from the removal of the technology without also having to deal with the personal backlash associated with taking the technology away. An advantage of infrastructurally imposed presence was described at the Central Intelligence Agency (CIA) by one person who talked about the opportunity for interaction:

> Well, none of us have the option during the entire workday of looking at a phone. You can see the impact of this at the Starbucks we have inside of our headquarters. When people are standing in line at that Starbucks, they don't have an option of a phone because they don't have a phone with them. Everybody in that line is having a conversation because their phone is sitting out in their car. They can't be reading an article or looking at social media. People are always talking in line.

This infrastructurally or organizationally imposed presence removes the pressure within as well as the pressures from without.[5] When the organization imposes entitled presence and no one is allowed to be on their phones in meetings or conversations, everyone has an immediate excuse. Everyone outside the organization knows that that individual cannot be reached while inside the building, so expectations and pressures for availability are reduced. However, in many cases, this type of imposed presence is not possible.

So both these issues are true. Communication technologies can distract you, and sometimes you can engage more when you are not distracted by these technologies. However, you are often in a position where you need to be reached to receive certain messages. A critical question to consider when deciding about entitled presence seems to be, Who has the agency to make a decision about information control, and when are you willing to give up that control to someone else?

WHEN SHOULD YOU USE ENTITLED PRESENCE?

Be careful how often you use entitled presence. If you are in a burning building, and you are the only one who knows the best way to get out, then tell everyone to turn off their technology and listen to you. In this situation, you have the credibility and the relevant information to command the audience's attention, and there is nothing that they will find more relevant to their immediate needs on their digital devices. However, you are rarely, even metaphorically, in such a situation. When speaking, it is important to consider what information the audience needs and what specifically you need from the audience. Once you have considered these needs, how can you construct an environment that supports both your needs and those of the audience? For example, you might ask participants to focus on you during a specific part of your presentation or meeting. You also may recognize the large costs associated with a face-to-face meeting and therefore dramatically limit how much time you request that the audience's focus be on you.

It is unrealistic to rely on your audience to just know that they need to focus on your message and to put their device away. Telling them to put their device away is problematic over long periods without being explicit about why and how the audience will benefit. Without this specific attention to the message, the audience's frustration can lead to the loss of your credibility and social capital.

As we discussed with budgeted presence, each type of presence should consider three factors: context, message, and relationship. Specifically, where are you? Next, what are you talking about? And finally, with whom are you talking? Consider your decision to engage in entitled social presence as it relates to these three factors.

Where Are You?

The contextual factors to consider are closely connected to the expectations and norms that your audience might have in a specific situation. For example, certain norms might be expected on an organizational retreat or brainstorming session, but only if these expectations are made explicit. As a leader, you need to be clear and consistent about your expectations. If you encourage entitled presence during your presentations but continue to send requests and set expectations for quick message response times while people are in other meetings, you may lose respect. These dual expectations make it difficult for entitled presence to be effective.

With Whom Are You Interacting?

When I ask people about entitled presence, they often believe that they have the right to ask someone to put their technology away when they have positional power over their audience. Often, people will suggest that they are OK or at least understand the attempt at entitled presence when the person has authority over them.

What Are You Talking About?

The content of the message can also contribute to the choice of entitled presence. If you are recognizing the needs of your audience and they need the message that you are providing, an audience might consider that you are doing them a favor. If you have information that the audience needs, they will be less likely to be frustrated or hostile if you take their technology away.

Businesspeople may fantasize about an engaged environment where everyone is sharing ideas, unencumbered by digital distractions. But be careful when you take their digital distractions away. The fantasy of an engaged environment will always be a fantasy if control of technology is the only factor you consider when trying to create an environment of participation and dialogue. We will talk more about this type of environment when we discuss competitive and invitational presence in the next chapters. Until then, it is important for you to recognize that persuasion was challenging before we had digital distractions. Technology just provides us with the visual reminder that they (your audience) are just not that into you.

TAKEAWAYS FROM CHAPTER 3

- Be aware of the risks to your credibility when choosing entitled presence.
- Understand how your audience will benefit from this information.
- Explain the connection between your audience's focus and their own goals.

REFLECTION

- When you choose entitled social presence, what is it about your message that makes it so important to your audience?
- Are there certain people with whom you tend to choose entitled social presence?
- What are the primary drivers of your decision to engage in entitled social presence?
- When has entitled social presence been most successful for you?
- When has entitled social presence created problems for you?
- How do you feel when someone chooses entitled social presence with you?

NOTES

1. Shawn Langlois, "Bob Dylan: Enough with the Phones," *Marketwatch*, April 18, 2019, www.marketwatch.com/story/bob-dylan-enough-with-the-phones-2019-04-18.

2. Alice Gregory, "This Startup Wants to Neutralize Your Phone—and Un-change the World," *Wired*, www.wired.com/story/free-speech-issue-yondr-smartphones/.

3. Kory Grow, "Camera-Shy Kate Bush Asks Fans Not to Shoot Her at Concerts," *Rolling Stone*, August 19, 2014, www.rollingstone.com/music/music-news/camera-shy-kate-bush-asks-fans-not-to-shoot-her-at-concerts-187632/.

4. John Simons, "'I Lost It': The Boss Who Banned Phones, and What Came Next," May 16, 2018, www.wsj.com/articles/can-you-handle-it-bosses-ban-cellphones-from-meetings-1526470250#:~:text=Mat%20Ishbia%2C%20CEO%20of%20United,walk%20to%20and%20from%20meetings.

5. Keri Stephens, *Negotiating Control: Organizations & Mobile Communication* (New York: Oxford University Press, 2018).

4

Entitled Presence outside
the Workplace

It might be one thing to tell the employees who work for you to put away their digital devices and listen to you while you are speaking, but how does that work for you at home with your family? Or with your friends? I have talked with many people about entitled presence, and there is wide variation on whether you should tell your friends or family members to put away their devices. Some were very cautious about choosing entitled presence. One man who had no problem choosing entitled presence at work felt uncomfortable about choosing entitled presence outside work unless it was about a serious topic:

> I don't know. Honestly, I just feel like it's a pretty authoritative statement. Even if you don't phrase it as such. Even if you're like, "Hey, do you mind putting your phone away while we have lunch?" It still is like telling them what to do, and I don't know if I would feel comfortable saying that to someone if we were planning on just having a friendly lunch. However, if I was planning on telling them something like serious or something like that, I would be OK saying that. But if we're just meeting up, I don't know if I'd feel like I have the right to tell them what to do.

Another woman said that the relationship she had with the person influenced her decision to choose entitled presence:

> It's never been with a person of authority, it's always been people who I have at least somewhat of a close relationship with, like I will tell my siblings, or I'll be very direct with them. I'll be like "hey, put your phone

away," or something like that. Or with friends, like, I might say—I guess I more say it jokingly, or in a humorous way. I don't know that I've ever demanded, just because, I guess I've never really—in moments where I've wanted to ask someone to put their technology away, it's been in moments where I feel like I couldn't.

Another woman said, "So I have only told about three people to put their technology away. Maybe only two. It's like they know but they almost blush. And they're kind of like, 'Oh, sorry.' But they're not that sorry because they'll kind of continue to do it later and they'll forget [laughter]. It's almost like they're a little embarrassed that I've said something. Almost like, 'Oh. She has a higher standard than I do.'"

HOW ARE CHANGING NORMS AFFECTING ENTITLED PRESENCE OUTSIDE WORK?

As discussed in the previous chapter, the choice of entitled presence can be an individual decision or an organization or infrastructure choice. You might have seen entitled presence within certain environments or ceremonies where there is an expectation that phones are not used in those places. For example, in a church or a synagogue, attendees might be reminded at the beginning to silence or turn off their digital devices. However, in these situations, since the audience has actively agreed to attend that service or ceremony, there is usually not a misunderstanding about device use. But norms for mobile devices are changing, and directions to silence devices or norms are not always effective.[1] I've heard of people texting during church, weddings, funerals, dinner, and sex. One neurologist told me that he was called to an emergency room to help a stroke victim. When he walked into the room, a huge sign said, "Turn off your mobile devices while in the Emergency Room." Despite the sign and the fact that the patient's right side of the body was numb from his stroke, he was still texting with his left hand and thumbs.

Many people argue about generational use of the phone and that younger people are more offended when someone tells them to put their phone away than older people. But universally, people talk about feeling disrespected when they don't receive someone's full attention. The real issue comes with whether you also feel like you have the right to take someone else's mobile device away.

One manager I talked to said, "It's just too hard. By the time I come home from work I am so worn out, I don't have the energy at dinner to force everyone to put their technology away. And I often need to take a call for work. So we don't really do that at home." As COVID-19 forced families back into their homes for long periods, the lack of entitled presence, or prescribed periods when people were not on their devices, often revealed how little time families devoted to conversation. One family therapist I talked to said about four weeks into the quarantine,

> This quarantine has been really hard on families and reveals the types of communication that takes place inside the home. Some families seem to be handling it pretty well. They are creating game nights and activities that they do together. But some don't talk at all. All of their conversation before the pandemic involved logistics. Who needs to be dropped off where, what laundry needs to get done by a certain date, what time a game or practice will be. Without practices, meetings, school, or appointments, there is really nothing to talk about. Everyone just vanishes into their mobile devices. They might meet in the kitchen to get food, but they take it back to their rooms to eat it.

The next section discusses how entitled presence is chosen within the context of friendships, families, and classrooms.

HOW IS ENTITLED PRESENCE AFFECTING OUR FRIENDSHIPS?

Choosing entitled presence means that you are saying that your audience should be prioritizing your content and your relationship over other messages.[2] While privileging the content is often emphasized when people talk about their work examples, outside work the emphasis is often on the relationship: "I can't believe he or she is doing that to me!" The closer you feel to someone, the more upset you might feel about the behavior that might then inspire you to say something. One woman talked about her frustration with her friend: "Are you going to cut it out and put it away?" I was like, "Do you want to watch the movie and come over or do you want to go home and talk on your phone?"

Another woman talked about the way her friend tried to make excuses for her phone use. But she never told her to put it away, even though the behavior made her very upset:

> I have not asked people to put their phone away. But I have a few friends
> that I think are very destructive with their phones. We'll make plans
> to do something like watch a movie or do an activity or something and
> they'll be constantly on their phones—or I might be having an intense,
> focused conversation over at dinner with a friend I haven't seen in a
> while and they'll constantly be on it trying to have another conversation
> and then, in a way of justifying it, they'll say, "Oh well, Julia's having a
> bad day, and blah blah blah." I'm like, "Who's Julia? I don't care." I feel
> bad for Julia, but you wouldn't tell me that. You're kind of using it as
> "That's why I'm on this phone." But the people that say that are always
> the ones who are on their phone. You know what I mean? It's not so
> much that Julia is having a bad day. It's just that you can't separate from
> your phone and it will have to be a thing that you're talking about.

Many people talked about being hurt but felt reluctant to ask someone to stop the behavior. The relationship needed to be really close to be able to say something. Another woman reiterated this point about choosing entitled presence: "I would have to feel really close with them to do something like that. As much as I like my friends, I don't think I have in the past or I would be comfortable saying like, can you put that away? Unless I had to talk about something that was very serious and I, in recent memory, I don't think that's happened. So I, I don't think that's happened before where I've had to tell someone, put your phone away."

Other people talked about how entitled presence didn't always make a difference in the other person's behavior: "I was dating a guy last year who was on his phone a lot and it was such a turn off, and I called him out on it a few times where I was very much like, 'you're on your phone a lot. Check your phone when I'm not here or when we're not hanging out,' but like, he was on his phone a lot and I criticized him for it. I found it very immature."

Some people talked about making a joke. One man said he would choose entitled presence only with a close person because he was concerned about being misinterpreted:

> Most of the time, it would only be someone I'm very comfortable with,
> family members or partner or roommate, something like that. And even
> then, it's usually kind of playful. I hate to be like the guy who's like, "Agh,
> put your phone away kids, rah rah," you know, I don't want to be that
> person. But it's always just like "oh, what's going on—what's happening
> on Facebook right now that's so wild," you know, "What's happening on
> Twitter," "Oh, you texting me? What are you saying?"

HOW IS ENTITLED PRESENCE AFFECTING OUR FAMILY TIME?

You might find choosing entitled presence with your family a little easier. Most people I have talked with did. Family situations are challenging because you have a house full of people and each person often has their own network. While the family is a unit, the people within the family are not really interdependent on each other for a specific deliverable or task the way a team is interdependent in the work environment. Some families might have rules for dinner time or for certain family activities, but many families don't have any rules.

Even without the rules, the frustration over phone use can lead family members to emotional outbursts that might not happen outside the home. One father I talked with shared his frustrations about his daughter texting and his choice of entitled presence: "No, she won't talk to me with the phone in her lap or anything. She knows. Far be it for me to be dramatic, but I tell her, I said, 'You know the 14th Street bridge? You're going to read about me at rush hour on the 14th Street bridge. I'm the guy on the hood of the car throwing your phone into the Potomac.' So, she says, 'You're crazy.' I said, 'I'm not crazy.'" One mother told me about how her three-year-old son grabbed her phone and threw it out the doorway. She figured maybe he was trying to tell her something.

Many people shared that since they felt so close to their family, the home was the only place that they felt comfortable telling someone to put their phone away. Said one teenager about choosing entitled presence, "Um, I don't think so because I honestly think the only people I'd be comfortable saying that to would be um, my, like my brother, my parents and honestly if we're having a conversation, if I'm having a conversation with them, I'm more likely to take out my phone with them, then worry about them taking out their phone with me."

While the workplace maintains certain hierarchies and norms, these norms need to be created within the family. You might say parents have a certain status in the hierarchy of the family, but that can be difficult to maintain. This status and "power" may erode as children get older. Telling your two-year-old to put a mobile device away is different from telling a teenager to put their mobile device away. Said one parent when I asked her about guidelines, "No, we don't really have those. I did when my kids were younger. But I don't now. My daughter was going to sleep with her phone, and I felt like she was on her phone all night. I think that has stopped. So, at this point, I haven't seen a reason to put rules in place. Although, from time to time, the one thing to get my kids' attention has always been, 'I'm taking your cell phone away.'"

The intersection between work and home makes entitled presence challenging if someone in the house has fewer boundaries between those environments. Many people talked about the difficulty in enforcing entitled presence during dinner when some people at the table might have to take a call from work. Or work could sometimes invade other activities and gatherings requiring the use of a mobile device. Said one parent, "I was at a children's birthday party last week and the puppeteer actually asked all the parents to put their phones away. Unbelievable! Like I care about that ridiculous puppet show! I have a bunch of work to get done this weekend and this is the perfect time to do it."

A graduate student from China talked about a recent family gathering, "We were getting together as a family to celebrate the Chinese New Year and my father told us we all had to put our phones away and talk with each other. It was really hard. No one had anything to say."

HOW IS ENTITLED PRESENCE AFFECTING OUR CLASSROOMS?

One of the contexts that I have seen most conducive to entitled presence is classroom environments. The classroom environment is very different from the business environment. Whether you are considering kindergarten through twelfth grade (K–12) or the university context, the school environment involves an implicit contract where the students in the school (or their parents) give in to certain rules and protocols in return for completion of a grade or a degree. Just like the organizations that we talked about in chapter 3, schools approach entitled presence from an individual perspective (through teachers or faculty), from an organizational perspective (through school-wide rules and regulations), or from an infrastructural perspective (where wireless service throughout parts of the campus is shut down).

Impact on the Faculty

Within the K–12 environment, rules and regulations about mobile device use usually come at the organizational level. One principal told me about the expense involved with taking students' mobile devices away in the morning and giving them back in the afternoon: "Sometimes it would take about an hour in the morning and an hour in the afternoon to have each student check in their phone and have it placed in a locker. Then we were also liable for these very expensive devices. At the end of the day, it just wasn't worth it." Another high school promised that they would confiscate a mobile device if a teacher or administrator saw it and the student would be fined $25. The students would not get their device back until the student paid the fee. One graduate student talked about how mobile device use changed since he was in high school:

When I was in high school, which wasn't that long ago, phones were like faux pas. You couldn't have them out. I remember one time I had—this was even before smartphones. I had like, a Razor, you know, Motorola? And I would sneak texting in my hoodie pocket at lunch, at lunch time, texting my mom, I was like, "I need to get picked up after the basketball game tonight," you know, something pretty innocuous, and the principal just happened to be walking by. (He) took my phone and was like, "you can get this back after next hour." It was just, you know, crushing. But now, after going to a high school for the last two years, working there, it's completely different. Kids just keep their phones on their desks the whole period. The teachers—it's a battle they're not willing to fight anymore because it's just thirty-five against one, it's not something you're going to win. It's just the dynamics have changed tremendously in the last five to ten years with that kind of stuff.

At the university level, mobile device use becomes more of an individual decision on the part of each faculty member. Over the past ten years, professors have debated about whether to allow students access to their digital devices in the classroom.[3] When I talk about entitled presence in the university, I sometimes get eye rolls from other faculty members. Many say, "Of course I have to remove technology from students. The technology is a distraction and they can't stop themselves."

The risk to the faculty member is not the same as the risk to a leader within an organization. While social capital and loss of credibility can be a risk within organizations, the university environment is somewhat different. In some ways, the professor's syllabus within a course serves as a type of contract that is mutually agreed on by the faculty member and the student at the beginning of the semester. The student agrees to the policies of the syllabus in exchange for college credits at the end of the semester. If students don't want to put up with a policy that restricts phone use in the classroom, they can always drop the course.

When I am teaching, I notice a difference in the tolerance for a professor's use of entitled presence change depending on the size of the class and the age of the student. The larger the class, the harder it is to enforce entitled presence in the classroom. Also, students enrolled in executive degree programs like the executive MBA or executive master's degree in leadership, who are balancing work and school, seem to lose respect for a faculty member that doesn't recognize students' competing priorities. Custom executive programs where executive students are taking a course for a certificate, or for a short workshop, have very little tolerance for an entitled presence strategy.

Regardless of the context, the entitled presence strategy still requires that the professor police mobile device use through visibility. This need for visual cues as a way to keep students focused was never more obvious than when university courses went virtual after the COVID-19 pandemic shut down campuses. University professors couldn't remove virtual devices from the classroom because devices were the classroom. One student talked about the changing situation: "Before COVID, when our class was in-person, my professor used to say no electronic devices allowed. You could only take notes on paper. But when we switched online, you have to use your computer. So electronic devices cannot be avoided. Of course, I can switch my screen to other websites. I open the camera and I stare at a camera, but no one can see what I'm doing."

Some professors tried to control technology by insisting that cameras be on so that the professor could see all the students. One professor required students who didn't have a working camera to participate in the chat every 10 minutes summarizing what the class was about to prove that he was listening.

Impact on Students

Many faculty members talk about how their students appreciate the restriction when the class has a no technology policy. Faculty talk about how students were upset initially but then realized the freedom of engaging in a discussion without having to worry about checking their technology.[4] Researchers have also found that laptops in the classroom were not only distracting to the user but even more distracting to the person sitting behind the user or next to the user.[5] The lack of control of the device can be distracting to people nearby who notice the changing windows on the laptop next to them. One student said, "I was a little upset when the professor talked about the no laptop policy at the beginning of the semester but when I look back on it I actually learned more in that class than in the others when I was distracted by my technology."

I was conducting a focus group of undergraduate students at Georgetown on multicommunicating and trying to understand how they made decisions about when to multicommunicate. One student actually wanted the university to assume entitled presence. She suggested, "The university should cut off access to the internet every day between 5 and 7 pm to give people a chance to talk to each other rather than be glued to our phones." Her suggestion points to the overwhelmed feeling that many people experience as they are faced with multiple options for presence every second of every day.

This same need for the professor to use entitled presence came when I talked with many students during the COVID-19 pandemic and students moved to virtual learning. While many faculty members were concerned about students and relaxed some of the rules and expectations of the virtual classrooms, some students said they needed the structure and rules to help them stay focused. While the students needed the technology to connect to class, one student said, "I wish my professor would have stressed the importance of focusing only on the class and not on other things. I wish he would have cold called students and forced students to keep their cameras on during class. My situation at home is very crazy, with my grandfather needing help and my brothers and sisters taking their own classes. I would have liked a little more structure to help me stay focused."

WHEN SHOULD YOU CHOOSE ENTITLED PRESENCE?

Just like in the workplace, entitled presence can be the right choice when you need your audience to focus on your content and relationship. The challenge is that the audience needs to understand and respect the importance of this need. So telling someone to put away their mobile devices should come with an explanation to your audience of why it is in their best interest to do so. Be sure to consider context, message, and audience.

Where Are You?

If you can't visibly see the person, it can be difficult to ask them to put their technology away because you won't know if they do it anyway. If they will be mad or frustrated by this demand, it seems pointless to express it if you can't even tell if it worked.

What Are You Talking About?

The content of your message helps to provide the reason for your audience to focus on you. Many people talked about the seriousness of the message as more important for entitled presence. If you demand the attention of your audience and then the person does not understand why you demanded this focus, you risk hurting your relationship.

With Whom Are You Talking?

The person that you are talking with matters. Think about your relationship and the value you have for it. Talking about your conditions for entitled presence with this other person can be your way of establishing norms and routines for your relationship.

TAKEAWAYS FROM CHAPTER 4

- Entitled presence can be risky.
- People do not like to be told to put their devices away.
- Try to understand the goals of your audience and how their needs intersect with your message.

REFLECTION

- When do you most often choose entitled social presence at home and with friends?
- Are there certain people with whom you tend to choose to enact entitled social presence?
- What are the primary drivers of your decision to engage in entitled social presence?
- When has entitled social presence been most effective for you?
- When has entitled social presence created problems for you?
- How do you feel when someone chooses entitled social presence with you?

NOTES

1. Gabriele Morandin, Marcello Russo, and Ariane Ollier-Malaterre, "Put Down That Phone! Smart Use of Smartphones for Work and Beyond," *Journal of Management Inquiry* 27, no. 2 (2018): 352–56, doi:10.1177/1056492618762964.

2. Jeffrey A. Hall, Nancy Baym, and Kate Miller, "Put Down That Phone and Talk to Me: Understanding the Roles of Mobile Phone Norm Adherence and Similarity in Relationships," *Mobile Media & Communication* 2, no. 2 (2014): 134–53, doi:10.1177/2050157913517684.

3. Sherwyn Morreale, Constance Staley, Carmen Savrositu, and Maja Krakowiak, "First-Year College Students' Attitudes towards Communication Technologies and Their Perceptions of Communication Competence in the 21st Century," *Communication Education* 1, no. 1 (2015): 107–31.

4. Anne Grinols, "Multitasking with Smartphones in the College Classroom," *Business and Professional Communication Quarterly* 77, no. 1 (2014): 89–95.

5. Faria Sana, Tina Weston, and Nicholas Cepeda, "Laptop Multitasking Hinders Classroom Learning for Both Users and Nearby Peers," *Computers & Education* 62 (2013): 24–31.

Part III

Selling Your Agenda while Screens Are On

Competitive Presence

You might not think of yourself as a salesperson, but many of your messages are selling an idea, if not a specific object or event. You want someone to talk with you, or go somewhere with you, or learn about something you know, or buy something from you. In this part, you'll learn strategies for getting your audience to choose your message instead of their device. The secret: it is all about them!

5

Competitive Presence in the Workplace

In chapters 1 and 2, we talked about how much time people are spending on their mobile devices. And then, in chapters 3 and 4, we talked about the dangers of demanding that people put their mobile devices away and listen to our messages. You might be wondering: What is the answer to the problem of the distracted audience? The answer comes in recognizing that your message has to be *all about your audience.*

You might be saying, my messages are important, and my audience will, in time, eventually realize how important it is to listen. My answer to that is you don't have that time to waste. You need to engage your audience right away. Why? Because your audience members are holding in their hand a device that will take them somewhere else, anywhere else, where they can find a message that matters to them more than yours. Once you lose them, it is very hard to get them back.

WHAT IS COMPETITIVE PRESENCE?

Engaging in competitive presence means you don't demand that your audience members put their mobile devices away. Instead, you create such a compelling message that the audience chooses on their own to put their devices away. Impossible you say? We have been engaging in competitive presence since the time of Aristotle.

Competitive presence is about using the rhetorical tools available to you to pull the attention of your audience away from whatever they are doing and focus on you and your message. I have been teaching executives about competitive presence for over twenty years. Specifically, when it comes to presentations, I used to talk about the importance of being engaging and charismatic. I talked about how speakers should be dynamic and use eye contact and volume and tone to pull the audience in to their message. But now your audience can look down at their digital devices and find content that is more engaging and dynamic than you will ever be. Whether it is a TikTok video, or an Instagram meme, or a tweet, or an episode of a favorite sitcom, it is hard to be more engaging than content found online. The only way you can compete with this device is with relevance. You must have content or messages that are more relevant than whatever they can find on their device. And when I am talking about relevance, I mean relevance to the audience and not to you. Relevance is what drives everyone.

In this mediated economy, where multitasking and "always on" norms create unreasonable expectations for what can be accomplished during any one day, your audiences are constantly trolling for relevance. To compete with those messages, you have to figure out what matters to your audience and focus your message on showing them how you can help them achieve this goal or purpose.

WHAT ARE KEY ELEMENTS OF COMPETITIVE PRESENCE?

One vice president put it this way, "When I'm giving a presentation, I know that half of them, at any given time, are probably checking their messages. So you have to be more crystal clear and nuggety. You're really competing for people's attention." Another director said this: "People don't read much anymore. In terms of a live presentation or webinar, you really have to be succinct and engaging in the way you present the information. It's really incumbent on the speaker, not on the audience." These two people reinforce three key elements of persuasion: you have to be *clear*, you have to *focus* on your audience, and you have to be *engaging*. Countless books on persuasion and presentations provide strategies and frameworks for engaging your audience based on the science of communication. In my experience, over the last twenty-five years of studying and teaching about

Review of Competitive Presence

Type of Presence	View of Audience	Goal	Benefits	Costs
Competitive	Investor	Persuade audience to listen to your message	Focus on clear messages, and the audience's interest could lead to more effective communication	Lack of persuasion

communication, I have developed some criteria to help communicators focus their message on their audience. It is similar to many frameworks you can find because it builds on these scientific principles. I am sharing these here to help you when considering your own messages.

Be Clear: Identify One Main Theme

You have the responsibility to give your audience a reason to listen. To compete with mobile devices, you have to focus very *clearly* on your one main theme that you are trying to get across. What does your audience need to know, and why do they need to know it? You need to be able to answer this question in one sentence. This sentence becomes your guiding theme or purpose throughout your conversation or presentation. If you can't answer this question, you are not ready to talk with your audience. It doesn't matter whether you have 3 minutes with one person or 45 minutes with 300 people. To create a compelling message, you need to answer the *what* and the *why* in the same sentence.

Be Focused: What Does Your Audience Need to Know?

Once you have answered the what and the why, you can build out your argument with evidence to support your message. This content and evidence should *focus* specifically on what your audience wants and needs to know. The structure of your argument and the evidence you use to build it helps to give your presentation focus. I have found that three primary structures can serve to support your presentation: a groupings structure, an argument structure, or a narrative structure.

Choose the groupings structure when you are talking with an audience that is open to what you have to say or who is interesting in being informed. The groupings structure is essentially three reasons why or three ways to implement your suggestion or solution. Let's say you are giving a presentation about *the importance of building trust in your team.* You might consider the three ways that you build trust, or three reasons why you need to build trust in your team. This presentation would be organized by grouping your reasons or ways together.

Choose an argument structure when you are presenting to an audience whose members need to be convinced. For example, you might be convincing an audience that virtual teams need more time to develop trust than in-person teams. An argument is organized with a problem–solution–recommendation structure. First you establish the problems faced when teams don't trust each other, then you provide a solution. Finally, you create an action step or recommendation that will help your audience implement your solution.

The final structure you can choose for your message is narrative or storytelling. Here, you structure your presentation in the form of a story with a beginning, middle, and end. In the teams example, you might tell the story of a virtual team, with the key lesson of the story being the critical role of trust in building an effective team. Stories can be incredibly persuasive because humans are storytellers. Stories can serve as the overall structure of the presentation or as a type of evidence within the presentation. All three of these structures—groupings, argument, and narrative—serve to focus your message on the needs of your audience.

Just like your structure is created for your audience, your evidence needs to be compelling and relevant to your audience. Evidence is compelling when it speaks directly to your audience's needs. The prevalence of data has provided you with the opportunity for complex visuals, but if your audience doesn't understand your visual, they will never be convinced by it. Your evidence should engage your audience with an emotion like surprise, anger, disgust, sadness, or happiness. You don't want to cause confusion, bewilderment, or boredom, which often result from an overwhelming chart with an unclear purpose.

Be Engaging: Use Your Body to Deliver the Message

While your content needs to be *engaging*, you also need to think about what you bring to your message. Your *body and nonverbal signals* are critical to an engaging message. Consider your tone, your emphasis, your eye contact, and your gestures. Your whole body needs to help you deliver a compelling message. This challenge became even more difficult during the pandemic when your nonverbals and body language were reduced to what was visible in the videoconferencing window. However, it means knowing where your eyes are focused so your audience feels as if you are looking at them. You need to use the nonverbals available to you in the video window to express your interest and passion for the message.

Your nonverbals often follow your own feelings about a presentation. I have found the first signal that a presentation is not going to be interesting is the apparent boredom or disinterest coming from the speaker. If you are speaking about something that you don't find interesting or important for your audience to know, then don't speak.

Finally, consider the role that *status* and *place* can have on how engaging your message can be. As we discussed in chapter 1 in considering the choice of budgeted presence at work, many people have talked about the choice of multicommunicating or budgeted presence as it relates to status. Many have said that they never look at their mobile device when their boss is talking or an executive in the organization. I had the opportunity to interview many executives in one nonprofit organization about executive presence, and several suggested that their organization didn't have a problem with people being on their phones during their meetings or presentations. Then, when I went to talk with the next level down from these executives, I heard the status issue come up repeatedly. One director I talked with in that organization told me, "Look, being on your phone in a meeting is a sign of disrespect. I know that. I try to stay off my phone as much as I can throughout the day, and especially in meetings with those guys. It really doesn't matter what they are talking about. You just have to look interested."

In addition to personal status, place also can make your message more engaging. I gave a seminar to a group of lawyers in a beautiful room filled with several mahogany conference tables. Not only did my status as the presenter help to engage the audience, but our presence in the room also communicated to everyone the importance of the moment. I presented to a similar group in May 2020, three months into the COVID-19 shutdown, and it was much harder to keep the group engaged. Not only was the video channel challenging; I also didn't share a physical infrastructure with the group that supported my message in the same way.

WHO IS YOUR AUDIENCE?

With competitive presence, the audience is conceived of as an investor. Think about a financial investor. She considers the options available to her and makes decisions about how she will allocate her money to receive the highest return. Your audience invests the same way, only they are investing their attention and their presence. In a communication situation, with so many content providers available, and multiple demands on everyone's time, a social presence investor will consider her options and allocate her presence or attention in a way that provides the most return on her investment. Presence investors have many channels available to them when making a social presence decision. They may decide to engage in conversations in physical presence, they may decide to multi-communicate by being in two or more conversations at once, or they may fully invest in an online conversation. When you engage in competitive presence, you are recognizing that you are in a constant battle to win the attention of your audience, and as a result, all your focus must be on how your message meets the immediate needs of your audience.

To be attentive to your audience, you need to be constantly ready to adjust your message. This means that you are constantly observing your audience and using feedback from them to adjust your message. One executive shared this strategy: "When it looks like somebody's attention is pulled away from me, I will focus on them and draw them back in. I use this feedback as a measure of how useful I am—if a lot of people are not paying attention, I use it as a learning moment—how can I pivot?"

Another executive talked about the importance of bringing in new voices:

> Instead of having myself run the meeting, I rotate it. Every month, a
> director takes responsibility for running the meeting. So, it's more of a
> peer-to-peer engagement with me providing some of the content. I also
> try to make sure that the topics are going to resonate for most everyone
> on the call. If not, I might do just a subset. If I have only three groups
> that something applies to, I'll take that offline instead of trying to do it in
> a monthly video conference.

Your audience is the central character in your message, not you. You should see the use of mobile devices in your meetings as feedback. Said a financial executive, "When people start looking at their phones or glancing down, it's feedback. It's implicit feedback that either I'm not doing something right or they're not into what I am saying—and while it's not ideal, it's also informative."

The visibility of feedback from your audience is much easier in a face-to-face, in-person channel than it is over a videoconference or an audio-conference. During the COVID-19 pandemic, leaders were faced with the challenge of exclusively communicating over video or audio. As the audience moves away from an in-person encounter, the audience has more power over the interaction. Throughout this book, I have emphasized the important role of visibility in monitoring whether an audience is paying attention. Without the ability to monitor cues in the same way, presenting or communicating via a video or audio channel can be exhausting. With the video conference, depending on the size of the group, you see some faces, but you can't watch their reactions to your message in the same way that you can watch reactions during an in-person encounter. With an audio conference, you can only listen to responses. Since larger audiences on calls or webinars usually mute themselves, this means you have little or no real-time audience feedback.

In many ways, this lack of feedback makes competitive presence over video and audio exhausting. Said one executive I talked with after two months into the global shutdown, "Spending my whole day on Zoom (videoconferencing software) is exhausting! I never know who is listening. It is so awkward to talk during these calls with a larger group that I hardly ever get much feedback. It is so much worse than conference calls because I am stuck watching everyone but not really seeing anyone."

I found this quotation from one executive really interesting: "The videoconference provides just enough cues to remind you that your audience is there but not enough to know whether anyone cares about what you are saying." At least on an audio call you can imagine that they are interested. On a video call, there are enough cues available to you to convince you that no one is interested.

Another executive told me about the way they generated feedback to keep the audience's attention: "During COVID, I realized my presentations had to be shorter and I needed to really try to incorporate opportunities for my audience to use the chat function. I realized I couldn't talk as long or cover as much material. But maybe the stuff I dropped didn't matter anyway."

WHERE'S THE CONTROL?

The focus of control in competitive presence is persuasion. Many communication strategies exist within the toolbox of persuasion that can increase the likelihood that an audience will choose to attend to your message over all others. In fact, most persuasion theories bring with them the foundation that before persuasion can happen, you need to have the attention of your audience. And keeping the attention of your audience so that you can share your message has always been challenging because your audience can be thinking of a million different things while you are talking with them. Some communication scholars suggest that a person can focus for only about a tenth of a second at any one time and that the mind works four to five times faster than a person can ever speak. So your audience must work hard to give their attention to you. In addition to their inner distractions, external distractions can also pull the audience away from your message. One of these very persuasive external distractions includes mobile devices.

Competitive presence is about making that audience believe that it is worth their while to make that kind of resource investment. And this contest for attention doesn't happen just once at the beginning of an interaction but also in every moment of your conversation or presentation.

WHAT ARE THE TRADE-OFFS?

One of the key advantages of competitive presence is the mind-set it gives you as a communicator. Knowing you are competing for attention helps you to focus your message specifically on your audience so that the message is relevant to them. We often organize our messages on the basis of what is relevant to us but do not necessarily go through the mental gymnastics to turn the content around to view it from the lens of the audience. As a communicator, taking this extra time can ensure that your presence is not wasted by you or the audience.

Another advantage of competitive presence is that by not taking the audience's technology away, you are not starting the conversation with your audience resenting you. You are not preventing them from receiving messages from their boss, a team member, an aging parent, a teacher from their child's school, or their child.

However, maintaining relevance consistently over time in a conversation or presentation is very difficult to do. Competitive presence suggests that you as a communicator need to continuously work to engage the audience. While the audience does have their technology and therefore the freedom to listen to you or not, at least some of the pressure is off you as a communicator since you are not holding your audience hostage from other messages or communicators. As a result, the main disadvantage of competitive presence is that you just might not be relevant enough. Then you have lost your audience.

We all have messages that we must give that might be important but not relevant. I think about this distinction when I am on an airplane and I listen to the airplane attendant talk about the safety features of the airplane and how to work the seatbelt and what to do in the event of a water landing. As you look around the plane, people are not even pretending to listen anymore but are trying use their last few minutes of Wi-Fi before the plane takes off. The airplane safety information is incredibly important, but in the minds of the audience, not relevant. Southwest Airlines recognized this challenge and used humor as a way to engage the passengers. You need to find a way to develop relevance to compete for attention. When individuals have access to their digital devices, they will probably use them. And if they are not actively sending messages, they are probably receiving them from other people.

WHEN SHOULD YOU USE COMPETITIVE PRESENCE?

While choosing entitled presence can be risky, choosing competitive presence is often necessary. I tell executives in my seminars when they are presenting to always be aware that they are competing for the mind share of every person in the room. Imagine that every member of their audience is receiving a text. What is going to keep them focused on you and not their device?

As a result, the challenge of choosing competitive presence needs to be considered anytime you are trying to focus your audience's attention on your message. Keep your messages clear and focused, and try to capitalize on your status and place.

Think about the difficulty of sustaining your audience's attention over time. For example, if you are on a video call or in a web conference, the size and virtual channel make it difficult to listen to the most amazing messages. So don't take too long to get your point across. Consider meeting length and potential competing messages every time you are trying to engage your audience's attention.

Where Are You?

The most expensive "space" or real estate in your organization is synchronous and visible space. Synchronous channels are channels that require immediate, real-time feedback, like face-to-face meetings or conferences. Visible channels allow you as the presenter to see if people are paying attention. These two variables make it difficult for people to do something else while you are talking. So don't waste this expensive space with a message that wastes everyone's time.

Ironically, even face-to-face presentations don't guarantee attention. One speaker told me about a time she was presenting to a group of architects about strategies for addressing the aging homeowner: "I knew I had a good presentation, but it seemed like I didn't have their attention. In fact, one guy was on his computer the whole time doing something else. He actually came up afterwards and apologized. He said he had something due for work but that he taped my presentation and was going to listen to it like a podcast on the way to the airport." So even though he was sitting in the presentation in real time, he was taping it to access later.

Recognize the role that a physical infrastructure can play to enhance your own presence. The more that you have the status and physical infrastructure to support you, the easier it will be to compete for your audience's attention. For example, if you are an executive with status, standing at the end of a huge conference table in a well-appointed room, the presence of the room will help you compete for the audience's attention. As you lose this physical infrastructure in video or audio channels, you will need to work harder to get your audience's attention.

When COVID-19 moved organizational work online, presenters needed to think strategically about the backgrounds that they were creating during video presentations. If you are presenting in a room where everyone is sharing the same physical space, the space is not distracting. Even if it starts as a challenging physical space—for example, it is too small, doesn't have windows, or is noisy—all the participants together learn to tune it out because it is shared. Not so with the virtual backgrounds. Your background is a character in your presentation, and the more people there are on the call, the more distracting the various backgrounds can become to the meeting. You are co-creating the space with the people in the room, so think about the impression you are trying to send.

I have studied telemedicine over the last twenty years, and one specialty I have studied is neurology. When stroke victims arrive at a hospital, they need to see a neurologist quickly to make medical decisions about their treatment. The teleneurologist appears on a video screen, and their credibility and authenticity is enhanced or hurt by the background they are speaking from. When the teleneurologists were sitting at a desk with their medical degrees framed behind him, they appeared much more reassuring to a sick patient than when it seemed as if the teleneurologists were calling from a dark basement with a dog barking nearby.

With Whom Are You Interacting?

Audiences have a variety of reasons for being a part of a meeting. For example, a sales presentation about a new software solution to a group of business executives could include some executives that are ready to invest, some that are mildly interested, some that are there because they are with another colleague, some that were told to come by a superior, and some that are there to avoid another meeting that they don't want to attend.

When your audience recognizes your credibility or status, they will give you more of a chance to get their attention than if they don't. If your audience is not familiar with you or your expertise in a specific area, commanding their attention and selling your agenda will be even more challenging. In these situations, it might be helpful to borrow credibility from someone else. An example of this borrowing might take the form of having someone else with credibility and status introduce you in a presentation or preview the importance of your message in an email or other form of communication.

What Are You Talking About?

When you choose competitive presence to sell your agenda, as we have mentioned throughout, you need to be selling something that your audience cares about. Or you need to reframe the issue so the audience recognizes the importance of the message. Your message needs to be clear and critical to your audience, or they will find something clear and critical to focus on in their digital device.

TAKEAWAYS FROM CHAPTER 5

- Construct your message so it is clear, focused, and engaging.
- Frame your message from the perspective of your audience.
- Understand the implications of your status and credibility on the audience's attention.
- Identify the implications of the setting for your message on audience attention.
- Consider how much time you can realistically hold the attention of your audience.

REFLECTION

- When you choose competitive presence, what is it about your message that makes it so important to your audience?
- Are there certain people with whom you tend to choose competitive social presence?
- What are the primary drivers of your decision to engage in competitive social presence?
- When has competitive social presence been most successful for you?
- When has competitive social presence created problems for you?
- How do you feel when someone chooses competitive social presence with you?

EXERCISE FOR DEVELOPING A PERSUASIVE MESSAGE

When you need to create a presentation that is focused on your audience, all you really need is about 10 minutes. I use this exercise with executives all the time to help make their presentations clear, focused, and engaging. So, let's try this.

Brainstorm

Get a stopwatch, and brainstorm for 3 minutes all the things you think you want to say about that topic to that audience. Don't try to organize it or outline it. Just brainstorm as many points as you can onto your paper.

continued

EXERCISE FOR DEVELOPING A PERSUASIVE MESSAGE
(continued)

It is *critical* that you keep track of your timing. If you don't, you will spend too long thinking about it and then you will abandon the activity. Now you have just wasted your time.

Consider Your Audience/Stakeholders

After 3 minutes of brainstorming about what you think you should talk about, it is time to think about your audience. Answer four questions about your audience:

1. What do you want your audience to do as a result of your presentation? The answer has to be a specific action. This answer will help you focus and decide exactly what you need to include in the presentation to get to this action.
2. What do they need to know to do this? The answer to this helps you to further focus what needs to be included.
3. What will this mean to them or why should they care? If you don't have an answer to this, stop. Don't present unless you understand why they should care about what you are getting ready to talk about.
4. How does your audience feel about this topic right now? This question helps you to focus on how you will organize your presentation. As I have talked about in this chapter, if your audience is supportive, use a groupings structure. If they are apathetic or against your topic, use an argument structure.

Take about 3 minutes to answer these questions.

Develop Your One Theme

Now you need to think about your theme: What do you want your audience to do, and why should they do it? Create a one-sentence summary focused on your audience. This is not a tagline or a mission statement but exactly what you want your audience to do as a result of your presentation (take about 2 minutes for this).

continued

Build a Structure

Once you have your theme, you need to decide what type of structure you want: groupings, argument, or narrative. Remember a groupings structure answers three ways or three reasons why or three steps. It answers a why or a how question. The argument structure sets up the problem so the audience understands it and then suggests the solution and the action step.

Creating Evidence

You will probably find yourself in many presentations using some type of visual—whether it is Prezi, PowerPoint, Google Slides, or the like. At this point, you can start thinking about the points you are trying to make and the type of evidence you might need to support those points. I sometimes suggest that you take a piece of paper and draw a number of squares where you can write out your key points and imagine the type of chart or visual that could support those points. These squares become a map of your presentation slides.

Introductions/Conclusions/Transitions

The final issues to consider are your openings and closings. The main purpose of an introduction is to pull your audience in and give them an idea of what you will be talking about. The conclusion is a summary of your key points with an emphasis on what the audience should do now as a result of listening to your presentation. Transitions are important to consider as you think about how you are going to move your audience from each point to the next in your presentation. They help your audience by being guideposts to help them see where you have been and where you are going. For example, a transition could be "We just finished talking about two main reasons why you should do _____, specifically [reason one and reason two]. Now we will consider the third reason to do _____."

This exercise takes about 10 minutes to complete. But if you time yourself and work through these questions, you will have a more focused understanding of why your audience should invest any of their attention or presence in you—which is your first step in engaging in successful competitive presence.

6

Competitive Presence outside the Workplace

Choosing competitive presence can be challenging when trying to pull your audience away from their mobile devices outside work. Why? Because when you are at work, it is easier to conceive of something like an "agenda" that you are trying to reinforce or sell to someone. You build arguments for a team, you develop a PowerPoint presentation for a client, and you create a sales message for a prospect. But outside the workplace, thinking of strategies to engage your friends or family to focus on your messages seems more like work. Persuasion still happens outside work all the time—trying to convince people to go to a specific restaurant, getting your family to agree to where you want to go on vacation, getting a friend to join a gym with you, persuading a child to focus on his schoolwork. But the problem is that your friends and family members always carry around a mobile device with them, so how can you get them to listen to you without telling them to put their device away?

HOW ARE CHANGING NORMS AFFECTING COMPETITIVE PRESENCE OUTSIDE WORK?

Remember, the goal of competitive presence is to engage your audience in such a compelling way that they choose your message over any message they are receiving. As you have read in previous chapters, people are reluctant to ask their friends to put their technology away. Additionally, if you are communicating about a message that your friend doesn't agree with, doesn't like, or is bored by, they can quickly go to their mobile device to escape your message. And they do.

Walk into a room in your home where people are scattered in chairs around the room. What do you have to say that is interesting enough to get people to listen to you? Talking about logistics can be easy. Do we need milk? Did you arrange transportation? Do you still have an appointment? In fact, logistics don't usually require much attention. Many people might think they can answer your questions while simultaneously texting with someone else or watching TV. But an ongoing conversation is different. One person I talked with stressed how much energy conversations require: "Talking takes so much energy. I've noticed it a lot on public transit. Especially if you don't want to have a conversation with someone you don't know. You just look at your phone. I do it at home too. It is awkward to sit there in silence without a phone, but when everyone has phones, it is easier. So I usually just sit with my phone."

HOW IS COMPETITIVE PRESENCE AFFECTING OUR FRIENDSHIPS?

With budgeted presence, you are on your phone and are not worried about anyone else's phone. With entitled presence, you have grabbed your audience's attention away from their device by telling them to put it away. So what can you do with your friends if you are not going to be explicit about asking them to put their device away? Some people have talked about humor. One person said, "I will joke, do you want to eat dinner with me or your phone?" Another person said they ask a little sarcastically, "Are you texting me? It's OK! I am right here!"

Many people have talked to me about the strategy of talking a little louder, hoping the person will look up from their phone. Another person said that she will find something funny on her phone and share it with her friend to get her friend's attention. "Yesterday, I was hanging out with two of my friends, and the only way I could talk to them about my day was to start by showing them some memes someone sent me on Instagram. They were on their phones, then we were all looking at my phone, and then I could start talking."

Ironically, some of the persuasion strategies (or what researchers term "compliance-gaining strategies") that are advocated as helpful can work against you when it comes to getting a friend's attention away from their phone. While liking someone is often considered a way to persuade someone else, many people have told me that the closer the friend, the less they feel like they need to put their phone away during a conversation. One woman told me, "When I don't know the person very well, or I am just meeting them, I might not be on my phone. But with my close friends, we always do it."

However, six basic strategies that tend to work in persuasion situations were also mentioned by people as ways to get their friends off of their phones.[1] These strategies include *rewarding, punishing, expertise, reciprocity,* and appealing to *internal and personal commitments.* Rewarding strategies involve giving someone something. One graduate student told me this: "When I come into a room and my roommates are on their phones, I have to get their attention by talking about a joke, or telling them 'you have to hear what happened today.' I have to start my sentence with something that makes them think that what I am going to talk about is better than whatever it is they are doing on their phone."

Punishing strategies are more common. Many people have told me that they walk away when friends start looking at their devices. One thirty-year-old man talked about his frustration dealing with friends on their devices: "I just stop talking. I stop talking and wait for them to look at me. Then they will look up and I will continue. But by this time, I don't even feel like telling the story anymore. I mean, what's the point?"

When you use an expertise strategy with friends, it is similar to the way expertise is used in the workplace. I talked with one woman who is an epidemiologist. During the COVID-19 pandemic, she told me that she noticed she got so much more attention from her friends than she usually did because they were interested in what she had to say about the virus: "I felt like I was just another commentator from a news program. Then when I started to talk about needing to get a new car and some of the cars I was thinking about, I lost their attention."

The concept of reciprocity is where you give something to someone in hopes that they will, in turn, give something to you. One person told me that reciprocity was a key competitive strategy that she used with her husband to get him to listen to her: "I try to model the behavior of not looking at my phone when he is talking and giving him my full attention so that when I want to talk to him, he does the same thing. Sometimes it works. Yesterday I had to voice my strategy and say—now I am putting my phone away and focusing completely on you because that is what I want you to do with me when I am talking."

Finally, appealing to internal and personal commitments may involve you getting the person to feel bad about themselves for using their phone and disrespecting the relationship. Or this appeal could also involve you reminding the person of the importance of a situation or obligation so the person feels bad about disrespecting the situation. These strategies seemed the most common. Saying something like, "Come on, I thought we decided to spend time together," or, "I thought I was having dinner with you tonight not your phone. I didn't realize you would be on your phone the whole time," or "We are at a wedding / funeral / birthday celebration, etc. Do you really think that is appropriate?" These are strategies you might use to make other people feel guilty so that they put their device away. The challenge with many of these strategies is that they often come with an awkward silence, where one person feels bad about not paying attention to the other person and then it is hard to transition to the conversation. One of the women I talked with said, "What is the point? If you have to beg your friend to look away from a device to listen to you, what does that say about your friendship?"

Some strategies people used explicitly addressed the mobile device, and others addressed the lack of attention or the feeling of being ignored but not the device itself. Strategies could involve verbal or nonverbal behavior or a mix of both. In the spring of 2020, I worked with colleagues on a paper in which we analyzed the use of mobile devices on the E! cable network television series *Keeping Up with the Kardashians*. Since debuting on

October 14, 2007, about three months before the introduction of the first iPhone in January 2007, this reality television show has run for seventeen seasons and features a California-based family engaging in what might be called their "everyday lives." We analyzed a random sample of 72 episodes from the total sample of 254 episodes of the show. Our research found use of competitive strategies 14 times, although character use of mobile devices during face-to-face conversations occurred in every scene of the show. The most common strategy was *questioning unrelated to the device*, where characters asked questions of other characters to pull their attention away. An example might be, "What do you think of this sweater with these pants?" The two other strategies were influence unrelated to the device, where characters said things like "Look over here," or "look up here." Finally, the last strategy characters used involved *nonverbal behavior* to engage attention. *Nonverbal behavior* involved characters waving their hands or moving around to pull audience members away from their phone.[2]

HOW IS COMPETITIVE PRESENCE AFFECTING OUR FAMILY TIME?

While digital devices have definitely invaded our friendships, things have become even more challenging with families. Some of this difficulty comes with the amount of unstructured time you spend with family members who live with you in your home. You eat, sleep, and live with these family members. If you walk around in your home with your device in your pocket, you are basically constantly in contact with your mobile device. The people who live with you become interruptions to a constantly streaming set of messages, from a number of different apps. While you might make an appointment to see a friend, you don't make appointments to be with family members that you live with. The closest thing that might come to an appointment might be meals. While many families have abandoned this tradition because of scheduling, some families still get together each day for meals.[3] When discussing entitled presence, we talked about rules at the dinner table that forbid mobile devices. However, for those family members choosing competitive presence, the energy required to get attention from phones can be overwhelming. Said one parent about dinner time at her house, "Everyone just sits around staring at their mobile devices. I want to start a conversation but it feels awful when you throw something out there and nobody responds, or even worse, asks you to repeat your point again."

A teenager told me about how frustrated she was when she was trying to talk to her parents about her college decision:

> I was really proud of myself. I had spent all day going through these college websites and I had narrowed it down to four schools. My parents didn't want me to go to a school that was over 5 hours away and I was trying to convince them that one of my schools outside of the 5-hour radius would be a great choice. I thought I had their attention, then my dad got a text and said he had to take it. I just felt sad. It made me think it didn't matter what I said. My opinion doesn't matter anyway.

While you have somewhat of a hierarchy within families, with parents arguably having a greater status than their children, the norms and hierarchies are not always clear. When I have asked people about the strategies they have used with their family, people stress how hard it is to pull their family audience away. One woman who works in consulting talked about her relationship with her partner: "I don't think you can compete with a cell phone. They're too tantalizing. Sometimes I will joke with my partner when I am talking and he is texting—I will say 'oh, you texting me?' we try to say or do something silly enough to draw their attention away from it, you gotta like snap them out of it or something. It's almost like they are in a trance."

One person said that they try to change the conversation, "Maybe if people feel like the conversation is going in one direction and it's not going to change, that's when people are most likely to check their phones because it's like, 'oh, I'll just pick back up where I was' and won't have missed much. So if you just bring some random topic out of left field, they'll be like 'oh, what am I missing now, I need to come back to this.'"

One woman working for the government talked about her husband's inability to pick up on her signals: "My husband is always on his mobile device. I keep telling him stories about what happened at work and he never looks up. He just keeps playing. When I ask him if he is paying attention, he just tells me he is listening and repeats something I just said. But repeating my comments doesn't mean he is listening."

The challenge with using subtle cues when choosing competitive presence is that the offending audience member who is spending time on their device may not even know or understand that their behavior is offensive. I was talking with a college student who said she often tries to get her father's attention but it never works: "First, I might talk a little louder, and then I might ask him to put his phone away—He looks up and insists he is listening—but I can see he isn't. I have stopped trying."

As a relationship becomes more familiar, the urge to expend extra energy to pull the person away from their technology dissolves. One woman talked about coming home from work after hours at the office and seeing her family glued to their mobile devices:

> My husband is usually playing a game on his phone, and my kids are playing video games or on their phones. I say hi and it is hard to get people to look up. When I try to come up with something to talk about, I am at a loss for words. A combination of a long day at my office, and their obvious lack of interest, makes it easier to just get my own phone out and relax. A conversation requires too much work.

While many parents complained about the challenge of talking to their children or teenagers when they had their mobile devices, I heard the same complaints from children and teenagers about their parents' use of mobile devices. Wives complained about husbands, and husbands complained about wives. The bottom line is that if you want to talk about something with someone and they are not interested enough in you or your message to show interest, it can hurt your feelings.

HOW IS COMPETITIVE PRESENCE AFFECTING OUR CLASSROOMS?

Discussing competitive presence in the classroom is similar to the discussion in chapter 5 about competitive presence at work. Faculty members and teachers, in many ways, need to sell their content to their students. They need to help students see a compelling need for the content.[4] Most faculty and teachers probably don't like to think of their job as sales, but there are many commonalities. While the student has already purchased the class and committed to a degree, you still need to get the student's attention in the classroom for your specific content or lesson. When students have their mobile devices or laptops with them, persuasion becomes even more important.

I always laugh every time I see a brochure advertising a college experience with a professor sitting under a tree with students gathered around listening intently. On beautiful days on campus, students have often asked me about having class outside. Class outside doesn't work well because it provides too many distractions. Now the outside has come inside the classroom, and every day is a competition with those distractions.

Impact on the Faculty

As discussed in chapter 3, on entitled presence in the workplace, many faculty members tell students to put their technology away when they enter the class, so they don't choose competitive presence. Other faculty members who choose competitive presence talk about using videos and simulations to keep students engaged. One faculty member talked about the importance of previewing material with, "This will be on your quiz," or "You can expect to see this material again during exams."

When classes went online during the COVID-19 pandemic, faculty members lost their ability to police entitled presence. One faculty member told me, "I have always made my students put their technology away when they came into my classroom. Now I can't. It is impossible to compete with all of that technology." A Google search that included the words "engaging," "students," "online," and "COVID-19" returned over a half billion results in January 2021.

Just as the lack of physical infrastructure had an impact in business organizations, the lack of a campus infrastructure had an impact on competitive presence. Many faculty members were teaching from their home to students in their homes. The abrupt move to the online environment meant that many students were taking classes at home with their siblings and extended family with a computer set up on the dining room table or in a closet. These distracting settings were one of many reasons why many students decided to keep their cameras turned off. When a camera is turned off, the student's name appears but not their live video connection. Faculty complained about the difficulty of teaching for a whole class session to a bunch of blank monitors with students' names on them. It was exhausting. Even when students turned their cameras on, it was still difficult to keep track of where each student's eyes were looking and if they were following the lecture. Some students noticed how much harder the faculty members were working to keep their attention: "I see how hard my professor is working, using PowerPoint presentations, projecting louder, talking fast. I can tell she is really trying. It is just hard for me to stay motivated when I am not in class." One faculty member told me, "When I am teaching to a computer screen full of monitors, I feel like the class can become a bad Netflix show. The energy is missing. I am trying so hard to engage but it feels like all the energy is only going one way."

The point about energy is interesting. In my own experience teaching, I can feel the energy of the room when I am in person. Not only do I feel my own energy, but I also feel the energy from individual students. As a collective, the class seems to communicate an energy that I don't experience when I am teaching to a room full of students online. Students talk about missing the feeling of energy from other students that helps them to stay motivated. Said one student, "I feel like I am sitting in a vacuum and I am watching and listening to the professor and the class but I don't *feel* the class." Faculty members have also talked about this missing energy. Said one professor, "I try to grab the student's attention but I can't tell if the students are looking at me or something else. They don't know who I am looking at. It is hard to keep their attention when you don't even know if you have it."

Many faculty members talked about strategies of teaching in 20-minute intervals to allow students to stretch and get a break from the video. They also used a "flipped classroom" model, where students were required to watch a video about course material ahead of time to make sure that they were prepared to participate in a discussion once they came into the virtual classroom. Or they might create blogs or discussion boards where students would engage in the material and learn it outside class so that they would be ready for a more interactive conversation when they came to class.[5] The challenge with any strategy that requires preparation from your audience is the extent to which you have 100 percent compliance so everyone is ready for the discussion.

In many elementary and high school classrooms, students and teachers had no way to connect in real time and needed to use asynchronous options. Some teachers used social media channels like Instagram and TikTok to engage their students. For example, a sixth-grade teacher named Tricia Zinnecker at Creekwood Middle School in Kingwood, Arizona, created TikTok videos about herself to connect to the culture of the classroom. They became so popular that students were making requests. She said in an interview, "The videos aren't meant to educate students but to entertain and remind them that she is thinking about them. When students laugh, and when you laugh, it builds the culture of the classroom."[6]

This use of TikTok shows how a teacher is meeting students where they are with technology so as to build a classroom culture that allows her to be more persuasive in the classroom. Other teachers have adopted TikTok as a teaching tool to reinforce the classroom content by also giving students a chance to express their knowledge in creative ways.[7]

Impact on Students

Some students expect faculty to entertain them during class. Students have said that if the class is boring, it is hard for them to pay attention. The mentality that it is the faculty's job to entertain can make it hard to create an environment where everyone participates in the learning experience. Many faculty members have pushed back on the idea of teaching having anything to do with selling. They argue that it creates a learning environment where the students become passive.

The difficulty of the classroom as entertainment mentality became even more difficult during the COVID-19 pandemic. The classroom, like the boardroom in organizations, contributes to an audience's ability to pay attention. Said one student, "The smell of the classroom, the walls, the ivy on the building remind me to pay attention to my professor and focus on his lecture. Without that, he is just a guy in his living room talking about history."

In fact, to help them pay attention, some students welcomed persuasive strategies. Said one student, "I really need my professors to push me, you know, maybe cold call, just call me directly to answer a question. Because for me, I have got no motivation. So, I really need a reason to engage, which is a direct push from the professor." Some professors tried to engage the students in the class by having students participate by doing presentations. While student presentations could work as a competitive strategy to change things up in a traditional classroom, many students I talked with said they didn't want to listen to student presentations online. Said one, "I am paying a lot of money for class and now it went online. The last thing I want to do is listen to other students present material that the teacher should be presenting. I don't want to spend hours listening to a student. I would rather watch a movie." While student presentations were not often successful in engaging student attention, guest lecturers who had expertise in a specific area could be helpful. Said one student, "The guest speakers really added to a change of pace and you also felt more compelled to be respectful of their time, so you felt like you needed to pay attention and respond."

WHEN SHOULD YOU CHOOSE COMPETITIVE PRESENCE?

Most of the strategies for engaging your audience that we talked about in the business context involve really trying to understand what your audience cares about. Then you frame your message so that you are focusing on your audience's interest. You do this because you need your audience to commit to some action that will help to further the success of you and your organization. But communication with our family or our friends isn't really like that, is it? You might need someone to perform a specific action for the good of the family sometimes—like getting someone to cut the grass or load the dishwasher or make their bed. However, much of your communication with family and friends is about sharing support or affection. Even sharing your ideas is often less about persuasion and more about helping someone get to know you. We will talk more about this type of communication in the chapter on invitational presence at home. But regardless of whether you are in a business context or outside of a work situation, if you are trying to get your audience to do something that you want them to do, attending to the needs of your audience is critical.

Where Are You?

If you are in a context where you can't control your audience's use of their mobile devices and they have them, you really need to think about how to be engaging with your message. Lack of visibility can make control even more impossible. Also, if you are in an unstructured environment (as in your home, or somewhere just "hanging out"), it can be especially difficult to engage your audience.

What Are You Talking About?

Just as in a business context, you need to talk about topics that your audience is interested in or frame them so they can be interesting to your audience. The habit people have of looking at their device when they are feeling bored or upset requires you to be intentional about framing your message for your audience.

Who Are You Talking With?

Sometimes the closer the relationship you have with someone, the harder it is to get their attention. When you are interacting with a family member or friend who has known you for a long time, they may not feel the same sense of urgency to pay attention to your messages because they have a sense that you will always be available. Additionally, the larger the group, the harder it is to maintain the attention of individuals in that group. Persuasion is difficult and it starts with choosing competitive presence.

TAKEAWAYS FROM CHAPTER 6

- Look around the place and consider timing when you are trying to have a conversation.
- Check to see what people are doing before you bring something up that might interrupt them.
- Identify how your status or relationship could be working for or against you.
- Frame the topic in such a way that your audience will care about it.
- Try not to talk too long about your topic without asking a question or pausing to let your audience engage with your message.
- Consider how you can use the persuasion strategies of *rewarding, punishing, expertise, reciprocity,* and appealing to *internal and personal commitments.*

REFLECTION

Think of the last conversation you have had with your family or a close friend:
- What strategies have you used to get your family's attention?
- How do you feel when you have to compete for someone's attention that you care about?
- Do you feel differently about competing for your family member or close friend's attention than you do competing for the attention of people at work?
- Have you talked about this with your family or friends? Why or why not?

NOTES

1. Gerald Marwell and David R. Schmitt, "Dimensions of Compliance-Gaining Behavior: An Empirical Analysis," *Sociometry,* 1967, 350–64.
2. Jeanine W. Turner, Fan Wang, and James D. Robinson, "Managing Atten-

tional Social Presence? Lessons from the Kardashians," paper presented at National Communication Association annual convention (virtual, due to COVID-19), November 2020.

3. Kelly Musick and Ann Meier, "Assessing Causality and Persistence in Associations between Family Dinners and Adolescent Well-Being," *Journal of Marriage and Family* 74, no. 3 (2012): 476–93, doi:10.1111/j.1741-3737.2012.00973.x.

4. Jeanine Warisse Turner and Sonja K. Foss, "Best Practices in the Construction of Attentional Social Presence: Securing the Attention of Multicommunicating Audiences in the Business World," in *Handbook of Teaching with Technology in Management, Leadership, and Business*, ed. Stuart Allen, Kim Gower, and Danielle Allen (Boston: Edward Elgar, 2020), 51–65.

5. Ted Ladd, "Why Flipping the Classroom Is Even More Important in Large Online Classes," *Harvard Business Review* Publishing, October 9, 2020.

6. Bill Barajas, "Kingwood Teacher Embraces TikTok Videos to Engage with Students," KPRC-TV, Houston, April 17, 2020, www.click2houston.com/news/local/2020/04/17/kingwood-teacher-embraces-tiktok-videos-to-engage-with-students/.

7. Alyson Klein, "TikTok: Powerful Teaching Tool or Classroom Management Nightmare?" *Education Week*, April 22, 2020, www.edweek.org/ew/articles/2019/11/13/tiktok-powerful-teaching-tool-or-classroom-management.html.

Part IV

Sleep Mode

Invitational Presence

"Sleep mode" sounds weird, because you actually need to be active in your conversations. In fact, invitational presence might take more work on your part than the other presence choices because it requires you to both silence your own device, or put it in sleep mode, *and* try to get the other person to engage in a conversation with you. In this part, you'll learn ways to create an environment where learning conversations can happen.

7

Invitational Presence in the Workplace

Think about a brainstorming meeting at work where everyone is sharing ideas. Or think about a conversation with your boss where she is asking for your opinion on ways to approach a sales strategy. Consider a time when you and another member of your team traded stories about vacation spots. Reflect on a team meeting where you and your team had to come together to resolve a conflict. These could all be examples of invitational presence at work.

The idea of invitational presence is that you have specifically decided to engage with your colleague in a conversation without being interrupted by someone else or a competing message coming in on your digital device. While many of these types of conversations take place face-to-face, they could also occur during a phone call or a text exchange. Your primary goal is not persuasion or influence (as we discussed in the chapters on competitive presence). Instead, your goal is to learn from your audience. Ideally, no one is engaging in budgeted presence (or in another conversation on a digital device). While your audience may make the decision to be in budgeted presence on their device, you have explicitly decided to focus on only one conversation. Also, unlike entitled presence, with invitational presence, you are not telling your audience to put their technology away. The choice is up to them.

I have called part IV's heading "Sleep Mode" to refer to your decision to silence your mobile device. Sleep mode—what does that mean? Sleep mode means that you have intentionally decided to silence your mobile device because you want to take the time to engage with someone else. Now, technically, sleep mode can mean many things, depending on the device you are using. Try not to think technically now, but metaphorically. You are putting yourself in a situation where you will not be disturbed by any other conversations or messages other than the one in which you are presently engaging. All your focus is on your audience.

WHAT IS INVITATIONAL PRESENCE?

Invitational presence is based on a communication theory called invitational rhetoric that was developed by Sonja Foss and Cindy Griffin.[1] So let me tell you a little about invitational rhetoric. Invitational rhetoric was created as an alternative to the idea that communication is about influence or persuasion. The goal for the interaction is for communicators to get to know each other, to learn from each other, to understand. With invitational rhetoric, you are inviting your audience into a conversation, but they are free to reject your invitation.

Invitational presence is an invitation for dialogue. You are not assuming that your message is more important than your audience's message or that it is more important than other messages that your audience might be receiving at the same time. While you might have more power than the person with whom you are talking, you are not intentionally using your status to privilege your message over your audience's message. The critical difference between invitational presence and competitive presence can be found in your *intention*. With competitive presence, you are trying to persuade your audience and you believe your position or idea is critical for them to adopt. With invitational presence, you are giving up control over the message but still sharing your ideas. You are sharing your perspective, but it is not the only perspective. And you are genuinely open to your audience's ideas. You are still sharing your own ideas, but you are not privileging them; instead, you are offering them for consideration.

Invitational presence can take place in formal, planned conversations as well as in spontaneous, unplanned conversations. Formal examples might include focused brainstorming sessions and collaborative discussions scheduled to generate ideas. We will talk more about these in the next section. Spontaneous conversations or unplanned conversations

Review of Invitational Presence

Type of Presence	View of Audience	Goal	Benefits	Costs
Invitational	Partner	Dialogue to create a fuller understanding of the situation	Understanding and relationship development	Time consuming/ Partner could reject your invitation

provide another context for invitational presence. These conversations might be initiated when you walk down the hallway in your organization and you stop by someone's office to ask them how they are doing or discuss a sporting event or a children's play you saw together.

This initial discussion leads to a deeper discussion where you share ideas or learn something new about the other person. Invitational presence could also occur over lunch or in a break area where people are drinking coffee. The common element of invitational presence is that the communicators learn something from each other. For you and your conversational partner to be open to learning in a conversation, you need to have established some element of trust and rapport. While your initial conversations about a play or sporting event are not very deep, they provide a gateway into a deeper conversation by helping you to make a connection and establish rapport. These initial interactions can also lead to a natural pause or silence. And instead of filling the space or turning to our devices when faced with an awkward silence, you resist the initial anxiety associated with the silence and allow the space to lead you to the next word or question.

A challenge many organizations have faced over the past several years is that, as budgeted presence has increased, invitational presence has decreased. Now when you are waiting for something, you use your mobile device to keep you busy, not to develop relationships and rapport with the people around you. No one feels comfortable breaking you away from your phone for an informal conversation. So the opportunity for the unplanned, spontaneous conversation is lost. One executive talked about this challenge in his own organization:

We never just hang out anymore as an organization. Everyone is always
on their phones. It changes the culture of the place. So, I started this
happy hour on Fridays where I brought in these great snacks from a
local restaurant, hoping to get some of that back. But people just came
down and got the food and went back to their office. Or some people
would come but everyone's conversations kept getting interrupted by texts
and emails. It has been kind of awkward. I am thinking of stopping it.

Some organizations have tried more structured team-building activities to foster relationship building and spontaneous conversations:

I think one of the other things that we've done as a team is, we've done
a lot of volunteer type things together. Just team building things where
we go and—like this afternoon, we are putting together bags of personal
care items for a homeless shelter and we'll spend a few hours this afternoon all sitting around doing that. Where we're all talking and having
an assembly line, but that is as much a team-building activity as it is a
volunteer thing.

Invitational Presence and COVID-19

An interesting development regarding invitational presence took place
when organizations were shut down due to the COVID-19 pandemic.
Before the pandemic, people would tell me that there was less and less
time for informal gatherings and interactions in their organizations. One
executive involved with conference planning said that the opportunity for
face-to-face networking diminished as more and more people were glued
to their mobile devices. She said, "People would bring mobile devices to
conferences, and I saw that the break-out sessions involved less and less
interaction as people would grab a snack and check their messages rather
than mingle with other people. There was even less informal communication during work time within organizations."

However, when organizations were shut down, people could no longer make any impromptu informal connections because the only way to
see someone at work was to schedule a videoconference. Then organiza-

tions began scheduling videoconference happy hours or lunch meetings to fill in the vacuum left by the inability to build and maintain workplace relationships. While they were popular initially, many people began to find that the informal videoconference meeting with no agenda could be awkward. Said one manager with whom I talked who worked in the fashion industry, "No one knows when to talk. When I tell a joke, I can't tell who is laughing because I can't read all those faces at once and I can't tell who they are focused on because everyone's camera placement is so different. I found I was drinking a lot more in Zoom happy hours because I never felt comfortable talking."

One manager who works at a financial consulting firm told me they started to structure their virtual team-building meetings with games or activities, so people knew how and when to participate. The virtual gatherings were different ways of building relationships than they would do in the office but still provided opportunities for team members to see and share ideas or stories with each other even though they weren't seeing each other in person. In some ways, the lack of opportunities for informal gatherings as everyone was confined to their homes highlighted the importance of this type of interaction among teams.

One leader of a school started a session called "Positive Purpose Huddles" during quarantine. The sessions were optional and invited people to meet and share strategies they were using to keep themselves motivated during the quarantine. She said about 50 percent of the organization participated. Another leader started "Wine Wednesday" as an opportunity for people to connect over video at the end of the day and relax. These optional opportunities created chances for informal, spontaneous interaction that helped to foster relationship building and trust.

Another executive shared that he chooses to start team meetings with a brief period of silence, lasting about 3 minutes, followed by a check-in as to how each person is feeling at that moment. It allows the meeting to start with a human connection rather than having everyone focused on their competing agendas. He shared, "The meetings are inevitably richer and more spacious."

Your digital device, with its endless notifications containing unmet expectations, can bring with it a constant impulse or pressure to produce or perform, removing the option or the sense of freedom to "be with" one another. Invitational presence is a recognition of this freedom and openness to what can happen in this space.

KEY ELEMENTS OF INVITATIONAL PRESENCE

The key elements of invitational presence involve you making three decisions: (1) you will focus on this one conversation, (2) you will communicate your perspective and invite careful consideration, and (3) you will try to create a collaborative environment where your audience feels comfortable sharing their perspective and accepting your invitation. What do these mean? It means that this type of presence may be by far the hardest type of presence to foster but could potentially be the most rewarding.

Focusing on One Conversation

I have been working on this framework for the past ten years. When Sonja and I first considered invitational presence, we thought it had to mean that you put your mobile device completely away (if the conversation was face-to-face). You either turn your device off or you put it away or leave it in another room. For example, one chief information officer for an organization told me that he would leave his phone in his office when he went to a meeting to make sure that he could really engage in the meeting. He said,

> I knew if there was a real emergency, someone would be able to find me. My secretary always knew where I was in the building. It really helped me to detach from my other messages and give 100 percent of my concentration to the people in the room. Of course, this became almost impossible when I got a Smart Watch. You don't leave your watch in your office. So I stopped using it. I wanted to send a signal that the meeting is important.

As time has gone by, and mobile devices have become more ubiquitous, I have found that fewer and fewer people feel comfortable completely walking away from their device or turning them off. However, they find other ways to signal, either verbally or nonverbally, that the present conversation is important. For example, they might say, "I am waiting on a call from a family member about my father's operation, and if that message comes in, I need to get it. But this conversation is really important to me, so I will take a call only if it comes from that number." While making a decision like this means that you look at the phone during a conversation to check on the incoming number, you will not pick it up unless it comes from the number you have signaled about. While this looking away can still be a distraction, you have explained your intent to focus on your present conversation.

The decision to attend to one conversation can also take place nonverbally. A government official who worked at the White House told me that he carried three phones with him at all times but that he always put them face down on the table, stacked up. He said, "I know it might have seemed weird that I had so many phones, but I wanted the other person I was talking with to know that I wanted to focus completely on them, even though I might need to deal with other issues, an upside down phone was signaling that I am only focusing on them."

Communicating Your Perspective

While engaging in invitational presence requires an openness to your audience's ideas, it doesn't mean that you can't share your own ideas. You need to develop your perspective and present it as carefully, completely, and passionately (if necessary) as possible so that your audience understands your perspective and has the opportunity to consider your view. You need to be clear about your own perspective but also open to adjusting that perspective based on your conversation with your audience. This mind-set, being open to another perspective *and* being open to *change* your perspective, is the hardest part of invitational presence—even harder than putting your phone away.

Putting your own perspective on hold or being willing to change it as you listen to your audience has also been connected to activities like active listening, empathic listening, and productive dialogue.[2] In an ironic way, it may be easiest to engage in invitational presence with people when you are not that committed to a specific perspective or when the topic is not that intense. For example, one manager talked about a conversation he had with a colleague that only happened because the wireless wasn't working at their location:

> It's funny, we were waiting for the meeting to start and we turned and asked each other about the Wi-Fi passcode. Since we couldn't be on our phones, we started talking about where we had just gone on vacation. I had been working with this guy for fifteen years, and I had no idea that his family went to the same beach area in the Outer Banks that we did. We are planning on connecting down there the next time we go.

This conversation is not controversial, involves a fun and relaxing topic, and has developed the relationship. Here, the manager didn't have to be open to a new perspective, just open to learning something new.

However, invitational presence and an open mind-set can be more difficult if you have a huge stake in the outcome. The more you care about a specific outcome, the harder it can be to be completely open to hearing and considering a diverse perspective. The Society of Jesus, a religious order founded by Saint Ignatius of Loyola within the Catholic Church, developed a system called Discernment in Common. It is used for decision-making and planning within the order, and it has also been used for other religious groups and laypeople.[3] One important element that is required to engage in this type of conversation is indifference. Indifference means that you are not tied to a specific solution or perspective. Indifference does not mean that you don't care. Rather, indifference means that you are open to all possibilities. This same type of indifference or openness to the conversation is important for you to strive for with invitational presence.

Creating the space and opportunity for invitational presence with controversial or challenging topics can be difficult but critical to developing conversations that can result in learning. For example, during the late spring of 2020, a horrific video of a Black man, George Floyd, being killed by White police officers captured the attention of the world, giving rise to a series of worldwide protests about the need for racial justice.[4] This need for conversation moved from the streets of our cities into our homes, our communities, our governments, and our organizations. Many communities and organizations instituted a discussion practice called listening sessions to bring people together to learn from each other's experiences and actively listen to each person's perspective.

Participants were encouraged to share their own stories about a particular topic, with the goal of the discussion being learning for everyone in the meeting. In the particular case of racial injustice, organizations scheduled listening sessions where they invited Black employees to talk about their experience of being a Black employee in the organization. Unfortunately, just calling a session a listening session does not guarantee that anyone listens or that anyone enters the conversation open to listening.

One director, who is Black and worked in a nonprofit organization, told me about an exercise that his organization was planning that involved the executive team (mostly White employees) coming together and inviting Black employees to start off a meeting about racial injustice with each of the Black employees sharing a personal experience of racism in the workplace. The director said,

> I want to be a team player. But I also just don't think that is right. What good will it do for me to share something personal that happened to me years ago? Am I supposed to represent the Black race with one story? I don't like to mix personal stuff like that with professional. After I tell it, I think it will only emphasize my race in the organization rather than my skills in finance.

For an organization that has never explicitly addressed race in that way, this exercise could be more alienating than inviting. Many employees might not feel comfortable in this situation—which brings us to the third decision for invitational presence: how to create a collaborative environment.

Creating a Collaborative Environment

Thinking about our example of the listening session, no matter how nicely phrased an invitation to a listening session is, your audience will not feel comfortable sharing their ideas until three conditions are satisfied: (1) safety, (2) value, and (3) freedom. The condition of safety means that your audience is not concerned about being punished or penalized for the perspective that they share. In the case of the listening sessions created for addressing racial injustice, because of the worldwide outrage about the death of George Floyd as a result of the assault by the police officers, employees might feel genuinely encouraged that speaking of their experience would not lead to later negative retribution. This concept of psychological safety has been described in workplace environments as the shared belief that you are safe to take interpersonal risks.[5]

The second condition is feeling valued. This condition suggests that your audience believes that you value them. Obviously, a big part of this within the conversation would be focused attention. Looking at your mobile device or texting signals a lack of attention to one conversation. So it is important that you explicitly express your decision to focus on this one conversation. Face-to-face conversations make it harder to hide your mobile device use. However, long pauses or the sound of typing in a video or audio conference also signal the lack of attention to the conversation.

Finally, the third condition of freedom is the most challenging to communicate. In this condition, your audience feels free to bring up any perspective they have and know that it will be considered and possibly incorporated by you in your decision-making or in the organization's decision-making. This condition is where the listening sessions around racial injustice could fall flat. Not only does your audience need to feel safe talking and feel valued by you, but they also need to feel that what they say could potentially influence your decision-making. They need to feel that you are open to learning and changing as a result of hearing this perspective. This perspective that you are open contributes to your audience feeling free to share their perspectives, whatever they might be.

Without this feeling of freedom, your listening sessions become nothing more than an exercise to fill up the day to make you feel as if you have accomplished something. Giving your audience a chance to talk, and then not responding to that conversation with action or explaining how that conversation is influencing the organization, could be worse than not giving anyone a chance to talk at all.

In addition to feeling free to bring up perspectives that might not be popular, your audience must feel free to reject your perspective. They can reject your perspective and it will not harm the relationship. This freedom means that sometimes you might leave yourself open to feeling disappointed or hurt by your partner's perspective. The director in the racial justice example was worried about how his rejection of the listening session idea would harm his relationships with people in the organization. This fear speaks directly to his fear of speaking against an idea he was not supporting.

While invitational presence can occur in online and in-person environments, the creation of a collaborative environment can often be supported by in-person, spontaneous activities. For example, I talked with the leader of a large, global religious organization who organized regular meetings of groups to come together in person and share perspectives about religious perspectives. While the task of the formal meetings involved collaboration and compromise, these tasks were supported by the relationships that were strengthened through interaction during meals, breaks, and activities outside the formal meetings. When the organization was forced to meet virtually during the pandemic, the task of the formal meeting sometimes felt awkward and difficult. The leader said, "We met last week in a virtual meeting that was scheduled for a couple of hours, but we finished it 45 minutes early. No one felt comfortable talking because the video connection makes it hard to talk out of turn and the energy was missing."

Another leader of a large nonprofit organization focused on educating and creating opportunities for members to gather and talked about the challenge of the virtual environment for getting people together to interact informally. He said, "It works great for information giving, but it doesn't replace the meetings where we sponsored coffee and donuts and people just got together to meet." The pandemic created a global opportunity for organizations to implement communication technology to support interaction and efficient tools for gathering. However, it is important to remember and understand the value that in-person meetings bring to the relationship goals of organizations.

WHO IS YOUR AUDIENCE?

Invitational presence requires that you think of your audience as a partner. You and your audience are working together to resolve an issue or solve a problem. The partnership perspective is important since building relationship and trust and exposing vulnerability are highly interdependent. With invitational presence, you need to be open to considering what your audience thinks. You are not only open to consider their perspective; you are also open to change your own mind as a result of hearing their perspective. So you need to thoughtfully choose the audiences with which you will engage for invitational presence because this requires intentionality and focus on your part.

It could be easier to engage in invitational presence with an audience with which you are not interdependent. When you don't need something from your audience in a conversation to help you fulfill a specific task or goal, it is easier to relax your control over the conversation. One manager talked with me about creating the opportunity for shared understanding in her team:

> I think it really is that every good manager is a good moderator. I do lunches for my team every other week—and I'll do my overview of what's going on in the organization and then open it up for conversation. I see myself as a connector. So, if something's happening in the one part of the organization, I want people to see that that could actually relate to something they're working on. So, they get a little information, conversation, and a free lunch.

Another example might involve bumping into someone in the break room and having a conversation about places to go on vacation; this provides the opportunity for both people to learn about each other without the pressure of decision-making since you will not be going on vacation with this other person. You can use this conversation to develop your relationship and sense of rapport with this person, which can benefit you in the future.

On the other hand, when you need something from your audience in a conversation to help you fulfill a specific task or goal, you usually go into the conversation with an agenda. For example, going into a meeting where your team is deciding on the location and time for the next retreat is a different story. You have a stake in this conversation. So being open to other perspectives is more difficult.

WHERE'S THE CONTROL?

Choosing invitational presence requires you to let go of controlling the conversation. Your mind is open to what your audience has to say. You also let go of control of your audience's mobile device. You invite them to participate and hope they take you up on that invitation, but you can't control them. One executive invited her employees to a day-long retreat, where she was hoping would be the site of spirited and lively debates. She didn't want to create a situation where she was in control of the conversation or meeting, so she started by saying this: "We are here today to focus on how we will implement our new strategy across the four main regions of our organization. We will only be successful if we all work together. Since it is not often that we are all in one place together and we only have today to work on this, I encourage you to focus these conversations and refrain from using your mobile devices for other tasks."

Another director of a finance organization started a meeting with a group discussion of goals. She said, "Today I would like to talk about ways we can give feedback to our clients. We have about 45 minutes to have a conversation about this. What are some norms we could establish up front as a group to help us to accomplish this?" Many of the members suggested silencing mobile devices.

WHAT ARE THE TRADE-OFFS?

The main benefit of invitational presence is the opportunity for you to learn and grow from a conversation. The biggest challenge is that it is hard to get your audience to adopt the same mind-set and put their technology away and focus on the conversation. A partnership requires a partner. You and your audience co-create the interaction. So it can take time to develop the conditions of safety, value, and freedom. It can also take time and energy to hear and consider alternative perspectives that don't agree with your perspective. In these ways, choosing invitational presence might take more time in the short term but be more beneficial for you in the long term. It is definitely more of a long-term approach to communication.

WHEN SHOULD YOU USE INVITATIONAL PRESENCE?

Three questions are important to consider when you are making a decision to choose invitational presence: Where are you? With whom are you interacting? What are you talking about?

Where Are You?

You can engage in invitational presence anywhere. But place is an important consideration for invitational presence. While invitational presence does not need to take place in a face-to-face setting, it does require focus and attention. Additionally, because you must be open to consider alternative perspectives to your own, it can require more energy on your part if you are interdependent with the audience or you have a stake in the outcome of the conversation. Also, are you in a situation where you will not have to engage in budgeted presence? If you are expecting an important call or you are in the middle of an intense task that requires you to be present in many conversations, you can't really put yourself in a situation where you can silence your device or put it in sleep mode.

One CEO of a software company brought his team over to Georgetown University to participate in a custom business program. I was facilitating a conversation with the team about strategies to consider when developing a new communication plan for their mission. Throughout the meeting, the CEO sat in the front row and engaged intermittently in the conversation while he continued to work on his computer. I asked him what his thoughts were on the communication plan, and he said, "I don't really have time to be in the middle of this conversation right now, but I want the rest of my team to talk about it." Unfortunately, the signal he was sending was that the conversation was not worth his time, which made the rest of the team question whether it was worth their time.

A director of housing and residence life at a university, in the middle of a stressful summer, discussed invitational presence and the importance of a comfortable space. Her university had just announced that due to COVID-19, only students in certain majors would be invited back to campus in the fall. I asked her if it was hard to have conversations with many of the irate parents who were calling her. She said, "I actually find the conversations not as stressful as I would if I was on campus. I can calm myself down and be open to listening without getting stressed out myself. I am sitting in my comfortable chair at home, having tea, and taking breaks to be with my husband, who is very supportive. Ironically, I have been more clearheaded and open to dialogue than I would be in the middle of the stress of my office on campus."

With Whom Are You Interacting?

You can choose invitational presence with anyone. But is this a person by whom you are willing to be influenced? One manager told me that she likes to choose invitational presence in performance reviews after she has given them a rating: "After I give the person their ranking, I let them talk about how much they don't agree with it. I shake my head and say I understand to all of their concerns and rebuttals. I think it makes them feel better to talk about it and feel like someone heard them." I asked her if she ever changed the rating as a result of these conversations and she said "No, I can't change them. They are already in the system and sent to corporate." While this manager thinks she is choosing invitational presence, she is not. She actually can't in this setting, because she can't change the ranking. I would argue that she is choosing competitive presence and providing her employee the chance for feedback as a strategy. The nuance is in your willingness to be open to your audience's perspective.

What Are You Talking About?

Invitational presence can involve any topic—from the mundane to the serious. Often, invitational presence can signal respect for a serious conversation. The difficulty or complexity of the topic connects back to your relationship with that topic. If you have a stake in the outcome of the conversation or decision, whether the topic is mundane or serious, it becomes more difficult to approach a conversation as a dialogue rather than an opportunity for persuasion.

When you are focused on day-to-day tasks, and are staying on top of all your messages, you can lose track of the importance of stepping back as a team and reflecting. Said one manager, "We're so focused on the day-to-day tasks that we have to do. We don't always step back and think about more the longer-term strategic things. And so our CEO is starting to think, 'What do I want to do for the next three years?' The last three years have been more focused internally. Now we need to think about external. So I just got my senior leaders together yesterday for more of a brainstorming session. It was really terrific to do that." Invitational presence can seem time consuming when considering the need to accomplish a task and the focus on efficiency, but opportunities for collaborative conversations and brainstorming can be productive in the long term.[6]

Many organizations were forced into lockdown for over a year during the pandemic. At the beginning of the lockdown, organizations talked about looking forward to getting back to "normal." As the time horizon for restrictions on working from home was extended, many people became

used to the rhythms of remote work and expressed concerns about return-
ing to prepandemic norms as new habits and routines were instituted.[7]
The pandemic restrictions have ushered in new opportunities for flexibility and the need for intentionality. In doing so, the pressures to approach
communication from an efficiency perspective could be overwhelming.
In an article I wrote with Bishop Brian Farrell, the secretary of the Pon-
tifical Council for Promoting Christian Unity, we argued that leaders
need to recognize the critical role that face-to-face, in-person communication brings to the development of dialogue when weighing the costs of

---

TAKEAWAYS FROM CHAPTER 7

- Put your mobile device in sleep mode so you are not disturbed
  by incoming messages.
- Make sure you have the time for the conversation.
- Be sure you have the mind-set to be open to what the other
  person has to say.
- Use active listening strategies like nonverbal signals that include eye
  contact and nodding your head or asking questions.

REFLECTION

Identify the three most important people with whom you work. They
might be important because of the frequency with which you communicate, the status of the people involved, or the topics you discuss. Write
down the name of each person:

1.
2.
3.

Now consider the last time you have chosen invitational presence for a
conversation with these people. How did it go? What did you learn?
Are there conversations coming up that require invitational presence? If
you have identified these individuals as having important work relationships for you, it makes sense that you should schedule time for invitational conversations. They can deepen your work relationships and can
provide opportunities for you to learn.

meetings.[8] As organizations make decisions about hybrid and remote working models for employees, intentional strategies for supporting invitational presence will be important to consider.

NOTES

1. Sonja K. Foss and Cindy L. Griffin, "Beyond Persuasion: A Proposal for an Invitational Rhetoric," *Communications Monographs* 62, no. 1 (1995): 2–18.

2. Carl Rogers, *Active Listening* (Chicago: University of Chicago, Industrial Relations Center, 1955).

3. Markus Friedrich, "Governance in the Society of Jesus 1540–1773: Its Methods, Critics, and Legacy Today," *Studies in the Spirituality of Jesuits* 41, no. 1 (2009).

4. Evan Hill, Ainara Tiefenthaler, Christiaan Triebert, Drew Jordan, Haley Willis, and Robin Stein, "How George Floyd Was Killed in Police Custody," *New York Times*, May 31, 2020, www.nytimes.com/2020/05/31/us/george-floyd-investigation.html.

5. Amy Edmondson, *The Fearless Organization: Creating Psychological Safety in the Workplace for Learning, Innovation, and Growth* (Hoboken, NJ: John Wiley & Sons, 2018).

6. Dan Ciampa, "A CEO's Guide to Planning a Return to the Office," *Harvard Business Review*, February 25, 2021, https://hbr.org/2021/02/a-ceos-guide-to-planning-a-return-to-the-office.

7. Lance Lambert, "Nearly a Third of Workers Don't Want to Ever Return to the Office," *Fortune*, December 6, 2020, https://fortune.com/2020/12/06/offices-covid-workers-returning-never-want-to-stats-data-2/.

8. Brian Farrell and Jeanine W. Turner, "Thoughts on Ecumenical Dialogue in the Digital Age," *Ecumenical Review*, June 13, 2021, https://doi.org/10.1111/erev.12598.

8

Invitational Presence outside the Workplace

Consider a conversation with your child about his worry about a group of friends he is dealing with at school. Think about a conversation with your spouse or roommate about a problem you have to address at work. Consider a family dinner where you would like to share information around the table about what everyone did that day. Think about a teenager trying to decide about which college to attend and talking to a friend. These are all examples of conversations that might require invitational presence.

Invitational presence, just like within the work context, means you need to enter into the conversation with the goal of sharing your perspective and creating an environment where the other person will share their perspective with you. While invitational presence conversations at work are often stimulated by a specific timeline or motivated by a need associated with a deliverable, invitational presence outside the workplace may have fewer deadlines associated with it. They contribute to the fabric of the relationship and in many ways are less oriented toward tasks or deliverables. Another example might involve a time where you are interested in having a conversation with a friend about a career change you're thinking about. Or you have noticed a friend who has been upset about a family member who has been very sick. You might be wondering how school is going for your child.

These conversations are important to have but would require some time to get into the topic. The challenge becomes getting that time. Unfortunately, just as in the workplace, because most people are in budgeted presence most of the time, it is hard to engage your audience in an invitational conversation. And outside the workplace, we often think we will have plenty of time for the conversation—there is often a less important but more pressing task in front of us. So we put it off.

Choosing invitational presence requires energy. For example, it requires facing someone you would like to talk with who is on their mobile device. You need to get their attention and then find a way to engage them in a conversation. Since your goal is not influence or persuasion or control, your audience has every right to reject your invitation. And it takes time to go deeper into a conversation to get to shared understanding. The initial conversation might just be getting you started with comments like "How are you?" or "This weather has been crazy" or something innocuous like that.

An example of what I am talking about with invitational presence occurred while I was on sabbatical, in about 2014, writing about presence. Faculty members get a sabbatical every seven years. I was dreaming of all the research projects I could finish when not faced with the pressures of teaching or service assignments. About one week into my sabbatical, we had a string of snow days together and my children's school was canceled for about five days in a row. All I could do was think about all the time I was supposed to be working on my research while trying to keep track of boots and towels and hot chocolate as kids moved in and out of the house into the snow. I found myself constantly in budgeted presence, checking my emails, or working on papers, and feeling more and more stressed about what I was failing to accomplish. My daughter Kate (about twelve years old at the time) was sitting on the couch playing a computer game where the player needs to keep penguins from popping balloons. She invited me to sit down and play with her. I am not good at computer games, so I have never really liked them; but I put my phone away and sat down next to her. She explained the game to me, and then we started playing and laughing about the game and talking about something that happened to her at school. This conversation would never have happened if I hadn't put down my phone and been open to having a conversation with Kate. In this conversation, we both chose invitational presence.

One woman I talked with who worked at a large nonprofit association pointed to this same kind of situation when she described a conversation with her son about the work sabbatical she would be taking. When she told him that she would not be taking her cell phone along, her son was delighted: "My son said that's the best thing he had heard—that I wasn't able to take my phone." As young as he was, he recognized that the very presence of the cell phone affected the kind of communication he had with his mother and decreased opportunities for deeper conversations.

HOW ARE CHANGING NORMS AFFECTING INVITATIONAL PRESENCE OUTSIDE WORK?

The major way that norms are affecting invitational presence outside work is the expectation that you will have your mobile device with you at all times. When you are checking a mobile device during the middle of a conversation, you are not creating a condition of value. Your audience does not feel valued or free to share information knowing that you will be listening. As budgeted presence increases in a family or friendship, invitational presence necessarily decreases.

It will be interesting to see how the remnants of the COVID-19 pandemic influence invitational presence and deeper interpersonal conversations. In the midst of the pandemic, we were faced with strict protocols involving face-to-face interaction where we were told to maintain 6 feet of distance between each other and wear masks at all times covering our mouth and nose. The inability to read lips or facial cues, as well as the challenge associated with hearing someone who is wearing a mask, may make invitational presence more difficult with people you weren't quarantined with when you are back to seeing them in person. These precautions provide an additional barrier to the mobile device to share a message with someone else.

HOW IS INVITATIONAL PRESENCE AFFECTING OUR FRIENDSHIPS?

Just as I mentioned in chapter 3, with the workplace, invitational presence does not just happen in face-to-face settings. Invitational presence can happen using a variety of channels. One of my graduate students shared an interesting example of invitational presence during a television series in China. *Sisters Who Make Waves* is a Chinese TV reality show that premiered in June 2020. Thirty female celebrities over thirty years old compete in groups. No matter what they are famous for, the women need to practice singing and dancing simultaneously. Finally, five people are chosen to debut as a girl group. The show presents how these celebrities live and practice together. At the end of one day, three of the girls were going back to their dormitory after a long day of practicing and are exhausted. They wanted to share their ideas about the day but were too tired to talk, so they texted each other the whole way back in the car. This mode of communication also helped them keep their conversation private from the directors of the reality show.

Whenever I talk about invitational presence, people always tell me the story about how they go out with friends and put their phones on the table face down. The first person to grab the phone must pay for the meal. One person I talked to confided, "The sense of competition actually really helps me. When the conversation gets difficult or boring, I am used to reaching for my phone. When we are playing this phone game, I have to stay in the conversation and it usually leads to great dialogue."

Great conversations or dialogues can often seem a little bit like fishing. I am not great at fishing, but I know it requires a hook to reel in a fish, proper placement of the hook in the water, and potentially long periods of waiting. I think conversations are sometimes like that. You need to be talking about something that your audience wants to talk about, and you may need a specific hook to interest them in talking with you about it. You also might need to be patient as you try different ways of expressing exactly what you are trying to say and taking the time to hear what your audience has to say. However, a good conversation can be very rewarding. They are often not efficient or fast, but they help to form the building blocks of relationships by creating trust and understanding. The mobile device can interrupt so much of this process, making it hard for a conversation to build traction.

HOW IS INVITATIONAL PRESENCE AFFECTING OUR FAMILY TIME?

My experience in my family and my interviews with people suggest that invitational presence is in danger of being lost within many families. To take the time to share your perspective and to create an environment in your home that promotes safety, value, and freedom requires time and building relationships. Over and over, people have told me about the importance of family dinners during the week, or Sunday dinners, where everyone shares about their week or their day. But I have just as many people tell me that they don't have time for dinners because everyone needs to be at a different appointment at a different time. Even when dinner does happen, because no one in the family is used to sharing information with each other that is any deeper than logistics, mobile devices become a welcome distraction from the awkward silence of the dinner table.

One executive at a large association in Washington told me about the time he banned mobile devices from the dinner table (obviously a form of entitled presence). He expected he would have lively dinner conversation. He told me, "It took my family about two months before we were at a place where we felt comfortable talking to each other at the dinner table." I have taught in a program focused on high school students for the last ten years. I have always asked them about specific times when they decide to silence their mobile devices. More and more, students have shared that they can't think of any time when they silence their phones. But when they do silence their phones, the topic and timing is usually related to family discussions. Many respondents have mentioned family time, showering, and sports. Some mention "important" or "interesting" conversations. But it is surprising how many students respond to the question of when they turn off their devices with "Never."

This state of constant connection can lead you to think that you are in invitational presence more than you are. When you send a quick emoji or a meme or even a text that says "thinking of you," you are not engaging in invitational presence. You are engaging in something that communication scholars call "phatic" communication. Phatic communication serves to connect with someone but doesn't provide any intrinsic value or learning. You have done this before—social pleasantries, small talk, quick connections. This type of communication can help you to feel connected to another person throughout the day, but it doesn't allow you to learn more about the other person or go deeper in your relationship.

Families, coworkers, partners, and friends find themselves rushing from appointment to appointment and spending most of their time talking about logistics or sending quick phatic or connection messages but never going deeper. These conversations happen in person and online. So while you may not recognize the word, you definitely recognize the type:

"How are you?"
"Great"
"What about you?'
"Great"
"Did you see that _____ [game, debate, weather, news story]?"
"Yes"
"Amazing"
"Yeah"
"See you later"
"See you"

Texts and social media updates can be reduced to one-word texts, emoticons, or memes. These provide a sense of connection but do not create a deeper, invitational encounter. With invitational conversations, you and your partner share things you don't already know. So stimulating your partner to engage in an invitational conversation requires your partner to focus on you as well as put themselves in the mental place to be open to a dialogue. This type of presence requires listening and attention to the other. It requires a specific type of concentration or effort. For this reason, it might require a question to stimulate the conversation or a topic that both people feel motivated to talk about. One person told me that they keep about five or six topics in their head all the time that they can mentally drop into a conversation to see if it can start a dialogue. You can also find games or sets of cards that people use to start a conversation at the dinner table.

These deeper conversations require attention which can be in direct opposition to your mobile device that allows you to walk around and get other things done while you are talking. It makes you wonder if the phones that used an older technology that were connected to a landline with a curly plastic wire connecting the receiver to the phone might have stimulated invitational presence. Maybe not being able to move around while on the phone helped us to stay focused. You can't do anything else. Invitational presence requires intentionality and focus, and it can be difficult or slow to get into but can also be very rewarding.

One study I did with a colleague asked college-age students about the strategies they used to influence their parents about an important topic that they wanted to discuss.[1] Parent–adolescent communication can involve challenging topics like drugs, sex, alcohol, relationships, and academic expectations. Research has found that teenagers who view communication with their parents as ineffective tend to avoid conversations with their parents. Fortunately for those teenagers, the mobile device provides a ubiquitous buffer that can help them to shield themselves from difficult conversations. We asked participants to think of a time when they had a conversation with a parent about a difficult conversation and it was successful. We analyzed over a hundred conversations and found that conversations that promoted safety, value, and freedom tended to lead to more productive conversations. Participants said things like, "My mom allowed me to share my ideas without getting defensive [safety]. She spoke with me as if she thought of us as equals [value]. And she didn't seem to be trying to change my beliefs but was considering what I had to say [freedom]." Interestingly enough, these successful conversations started with the participant talking about finding a "good place to talk" where they could have privacy or not be interrupted. Critical to the success of these conversations was the fostering of invitational presence.

During COVID-19, many families found themselves with much more time together than they were used to having. Some families transitioned well to the quarantine, with game nights or watching movies together. But for some, the transition was painful and took time. One therapist told me that many of the families that she was seeing talked about how everyone would come down to the kitchen, get their food, and then return to another part of the house to eat it. She said, "Many families live together but don't know how to talk together."

My family started taking walks each day together for exercise. My daughter by this time was eighteen, my oldest son Michael was twenty, and my youngest son Andrew was seventeen. I was working on these ideas about presence, and I noticed that our walks became great environments for invitational presence and deeper conversations. One person would take a phone as a pedometer, and we would spend the walk talking. Sometimes, the conversations were very light, and sometimes they were more involved. I noticed that walking each day gave us the type of practice we needed to have invitational conversations. As the pandemic lasted into the winter months and the weather became colder, we stopped taking walks. I could tell the difference in our conversations and the opportunity we took for invitational presence when we weren't sharing the walks. While I would try to start conversations in the house, there were many more distractions in the house and visible reminders of tasks that needed to be accomplished. These distractions and reminders made it hard for us to engage in invitational presence.

HOW IS INVITATIONAL PRESENCE AFFECTING OUR CLASSROOMS?

In classrooms around the globe, from kindergarten through university, invitational presence can create interesting opportunities for dialogue.

Impact on the Faculty

Invitational presence is an important element of learning. Learning in the classroom, whether it is in a kindergarten through twelfth-grade classroom or in a university classroom, involves faculty and teachers co-creating knowledge with students. If I teach a course and have not learned new ways of thinking about frameworks and theories as a result of conversation during class time, I have failed. I have many interesting experiences of invitational presence in my classroom. One of the courses I taught involved a principal who was trying to come up with a way to tell parents that he was canceling kindergarten graduation. Why? Because it was out of control. The parents were pushing each other to get pictures, some parents rented limos, huge balloons were brought in. Everyone in the class was appalled by the story. That seemed over the top for kindergarten graduation. Yes, everyone agreed. Cancel it. That is crazy. Then one other principal stood up and said, "You can't cancel graduation. Many parents might be acting like that because it might be the only graduation that they ever see." She taught at a nearby school, and both schools were located in an area of Washington where the socioeconomic situation was challenging and violence was very common. I have never forgotten that story. It would never have happened if I was in competitive presence mode and the whole class was my show. It only happened because some of the students decided to participate in a conversation about our topic and I helped to facilitate an opportunity for that to happen. I try to remember this story because I am all about control and worry about planning every single second of the class. But with all that control, I lose the opportunity to get to know the students in the class and how they are engaging in its work.

Discussion and dialogue within a class requires a partnership. To get to this partnership and invitational presence, faculty need to approach the class or a specific portion of the class with the desire to share a perspective but not control the story.[2] Many elements of the flipped classroom that we discussed in chapter 6 are using an invitational approach. Remember that invitational presence is not about control or persuasion but about sharing ideas. Additionally, as a faculty member, I need to help to create an environment that will make it easier for my students to share since traditionally, faculty are in a higher power position in the classroom. In this way, faculty have to be intentional about creating conditions of safety, value, and freedom in the classroom.

During COVID-19, creating safety, value, and freedom conditions was different in a virtual context. For example, classes taking place over videoconference provided a window into the home environments of both the faculty and the students. Just like the business context described in the previous chapter shared the example where the CEO seemed more approachable at the consulting company, students found that faculty shared more informal information about their lives during a videoconference class than in the more formal settings of the in-person classroom. However, the challenges with interrupting individuals during the video environment and the inconsistency in whether students were visible on the screen because of bandwidth challenges could make creating an invitational classroom environment difficult.

Impact on Students

Many students have shared with me that invitational presence can be difficult on campus. Students talk about the difficulty of getting to know people and make new friends when they leave high school and get to college. Mobile devices make informal conversation difficult. I grew up in Louisville and went to college at the University of Dayton in Ohio. At that time, I had no Facebook or Instagram or email to maintain connections with people from home. If I talked on the phone, I had to stand next to the phone in my room and couldn't carry it around with me. Therefore, meeting new friends and getting to know people were requirements of being a freshman. I would go to class and talk with other people before class started to find out who they were, where they were from, and what they liked to do. One focus group of college students shared a very different experience of college. They talked about how invitational presence was hard. Said one student, "It was OK for about a week into school to interrupt people on their technology and say hello, but after that, you just didn't do it. The norm became that people entered the classroom and used their digital devices to connect with people while waiting for the class to start."

Said another, "I just don't want to bother someone if they are on their phone." One student said, "When I want to meet people, I put my phone

away, but then I just end up standing there looking around while everyone else is focused on their phone. It is really hard."

During the COVID-19 semesters, when students were taking classes
online, some faculty members used a "breakout room" function as a way
for students in a large, lecture-style class to discuss a topic with each
other. The students would meet in person for the larger class in a main
videoconference area and then the professor would send students to individual breakout rooms of four to six students to enable them to share
ideas with each other. The professor would then bring them back after
about 15 minutes to the larger group. The faculty were trying to create an
invitational opportunity for sharing; but in some situations, because the
students didn't know each other, were not being monitored during the
breakout session, and felt uncomfortable sharing, they didn't talk. Said
one undergraduate, "During my 50-minute class, I was sent to a breakout session twice for 15 minutes each. When we got in there, we just sat
there. People started visibly looking at their phones while on video. After a
while, everyone just turned off their cameras. We just waited around until
the professor called us back in. What a waste."

It's not that the feature of breakout rooms can't work. But for invitational presence to be created, you need to create conditions of safety,
value, and freedom. In this situation, the students did not feel comfortable sharing their perspective with five other students that they didn't
really know (not safe), the professor or a teaching assistant was not there
to guide the conversation (not valued), and the norm created by the first
breakout session guided behavior in all future sessions (not free to talk).

Some students have suggested that visiting a professor's virtual office hours creates a much more invitational environment than going to
a professor's actual physical office. Many graduate students in my study
of their experience with suddenly online school confirmed they appreci-
ated virtual office hours.[3] Said one student, "When I visit in virtual office
hours, I don't feel the same pressure or intensity that I do when I would
go to my professor's office last semester. I am in my comfortable space
and I feel like we are on more equal footing."

Students in some of my classes who were not native English

speakers said that the virtual classroom was difficult to participate in. Some of the students had come to the United States to have the opportunity to immerse themselves in an English-speaking graduate program and were now sitting in an apartment by themselves throughout most of the day and only had the opportunity to speak English during their classes—about once or twice a week. The lack of practice speaking in English and the difficulty in navigating muting oneself and trying to find an opening in the conversation made the environment less safe for conversation. Informal environments were even harder, because at least with the class, the readings and syllabus had prepared students for a specific topic. During an informal gathering of graduate students, topics jumped around from movies, to books, to current events, to the weather, to the pandemic. This movement from topic to topic made it even harder for students to jump into the conversation.

WHEN SHOULD YOU CHOOSE INVITATIONAL PRESENCE?

Consider three questions when choosing invitational presence: Where are you? Who are you with? What are you talking about?

Where Are You?

Invitational presence requires a space where everyone feels comfortable sharing, and you need to have enough time to have a conversation. The setting doesn't have to be formal or structured. I once had to wait in line with two of my children in New York City for 2 hours in the rain to get into a restaurant that served gigantic shakes that were popular on Instagram. My daughter had heard about it. When I reluctantly joined the line, I asked Kate and Michael how much battery they had left in their phone. Wouldn't it be horrible if we got to the front of the line and our phones were dead and we couldn't take a picture of our food? They immediately turned off their phones. As a result, we spent 2 hours talking in the rain outside of a restaurant—and had a great time sharing stories. We would never have done that if we were all focused on our devices. When I asked them about their favorite part of the trip, they talked about waiting in line for the restaurant. Invitational presence requires a commitment to time and a commitment to your audience—but it can happen in a variety of settings.

You should not choose invitational presence all the time. No one has that kind of time available. But be careful that you don't trick yourself into thinking you are choosing invitational when you are not. Just asking for feedback is not enough. You need to be open to hearing it.

What Are You Talking About?

While competitive presence is very easy for me to talk about because I think and teach about persuasive strategies, invitational presence is not. With competitive presence, you have a goal that you are interested in accomplishing and you are trying to persuade the audience so as to further that goal. Invitational presence is an invitation for others to interact with no preconceptions of how that interaction will develop, no goal for persuasion, and no expectations for how the audience will react. Communicators choose invitational presence to grow in the understanding of others. Invitational presence requires genuine curiosity about the people around you and the perspectives that they bring, even if those perspectives are different from yours. Communication is seen as a means through which relationships are developed.

Invitational presence deliberately seeks variety, newness, surprise, and even what might be uncomfortable in an interaction. Curiosity and learning are more important than accomplishment of a specific objective or achievement of a persuasive goal.

Invitational presence might be thought of as on the other end of the continuum of budgeted presence. In budgeted presence, you are trying to make sure that you use your time efficiently. With invitational presence, there is a good chance that you could waste time or be inefficient with your time since you are not in control in the interaction. Everyone wants the positive aspects of what can happen during invitational presence—new ideas, a deeper understanding, learning—but these outcomes are

never guaranteed. And with all the devices we have available, it is sometimes hard to figure out how to engage in invitational presence and create
an environment where other people would choose invitational presence
as well.

There are many examples of forced invitational presence that do not
play out well. For example, you can see the challenge of creating an environment of invitational presence at the family dinner table. A parent is
frustrated that the family is sitting around the table engrossed in their
digital devices while eating. So she demands that everyone put their technology away (entitled presence) and share information about their day.
She can get the technology removed from the situation, but she can't
guarantee that a deep and engaging conversation will ensue.

Who Are You Talking With?

With invitational presence, the audience is conceived as a partner. All
members have an equal role in engaging in the conversation. In fact, it
is difficult to maintain a distinction between the communicator and the
audience because no one person's ideas are privileged and no one person
has primary influence over or responsibility for the nature of the relationship that is created. While one person might have access to more information or perspectives than someone else, no one person's perspective or
ideas are viewed as superior.

TAKEAWAYS FROM CHAPTER 8

- Put your mobile device in sleep mode so you are not disturbed by
  incoming messages.
- Make sure you have the time for the conversation.
- Be ready to share your perspective without the intent to persuade.
- Be sure you have the mind-set to be open to what the other person
  has to say.
- Use active listening strategies like providing and observing nonverbals
  that include eye contact and nodding your head or asking questions.
- Develop a sense of curiosity about the people that you are closest to
  and think of questions you might like to ask them.

EXERCISE

1. Choose someone in your life with whom you would like to deepen your relationship. Once you have identified this person, commit to spending 30 minutes of time with them with no specific goal other than to get to know them better. Prepare yourself with a few questions you can use to engage this person in a conversation. You may experience some awkward silences, but don't be discouraged. Conversations can take time.

2. Look at an analog clockface. Imagine that this clock depicts a 12-hour period of waking hours. How much time did you find yesterday for invitational presence? (Remember, you weren't on your phone and you weren't trying to persuade or change someone's mind).

NOTES

1. Katrina Pariera and Jeanine W. Turner, "Invitational Rhetoric between Parents and Adolescents: Strategies for Successful Communication," *Journal of Family Communication* 103, no. 3 (2020): 175–88, doi:10.1080/15267431.2020.1729157.

2. Sonja K. Foss and Karen A. Foss, *Inviting Transformation: Presentational Speaking for a Changing World, Fourth Edition* (Long Grove, IL: Waveland Press, 2012).

3. Jeanine W. Turner, Fan Wang, and N. Lamar Reinsch Jr., "How to Be Socially Present When the Class Becomes Suddenly Distant," *Journal of Literacy and Technology* 21, no. 2 (2020): 76–101.

Conclusion

Implementing These Strategies in Any Setting

Each type of presence described in this book explores a snapshot in time. It examines the elements to consider when you are making a decision to choose a specific type of presence to engage your audience. But conversations are ongoing—they are interactive, they are dynamic. These choices evolve and change based on the needs of the conversation. A choice you might make in one moment influences a choice someone else makes in the next moment, which in turn will influence you. While you might choose one type of presence and stay with it throughout a conversation, it is more likely that you will choose a type of presence on a moment-by-moment basis. Additionally, the choices are stretched more on a continuum than being discrete categories with a wide range of options for implementing that choice. For example, you could yell at someone to put their phone down and listen to you and you could also suggest at the beginning of a meeting that everyone silence their mobile devices so that they can focus on the meeting. Both these examples illustrate entitled presence, but one is obviously more emotional and directive and the other is more suggestive.

One of the biggest challenges in choosing presence in conversations is that what matters to you is not necessarily what matters to your audience. Your priorities are not their priorities. For example, you could tell your audience to put their mobile devices away, but there is no guarantee that they will do so, because they may need to respond to another message. Or someone could ask you to put your mobile device away, but you need to be in budgeted presence because you have to respond to a colleague

How Do I Choose My Presence?

Context	Message	Audience
How am I expected to behave? *Communication norms*	How emotional is the topic? *Sensitive*	Do I value the relationship? *Value*
Will I need to respond? How fast? *Response expectations*	How important is the topic? *Salience*	Do I have power in the relationship? *Status*
Can my audience see me? *Visibility*	How difficult is the topic to explain? *Complexity*	Do we need each other? *Interdependence*
How much time do I have? *Time*	What is your goal? *Goal*	–
How big is your audience? *Size*	–	–

who needs your information for an important client. Most problems with mobile device use are the result of a mismatch between what one communicator wants and what the other communicator is willing to do.

So how do you make a decision about presence when you are juggling all these options? When considering the appropriate type of presence to choose in a specific situation, you should consider context, message, and audience. Context refers to the timing and place of the conversation as well as the norms involved. Message refers to the sensitivity or the complexity of what you are talking about. And finally, your audience refers to the person or audience you are talking with and their relationship with you. In this chapter, I talk about each of these elements as they relate to your choices and what to consider when making one choice over another (see table above).

WHAT IS THE CONTEXT?

Context is an important element to consider. Context refers to the situation and space surrounding the message and the people with whom you are communicating. These include the norms of the situation, response expectations, visibility, and size. These elements basically answer the following questions:

- Where are you?
- How soon do you need to respond?
- Can anyone see you?
- Do you have time?
- How big is your audience?

Where Are You?

You need to identify the norms of the situation. How are people expected to act? There are certain situations where using your mobile device during a conversation might be unacceptable or frowned on. While those situations and places might change based on the people you are surrounded by, you should observe your surroundings to see what presence choice makes sense. Norms vary considerably from one organization to another and from one family to another. One manager told me about a time she was invited to her boyfriend's house for Thanksgiving dinner. Throughout the dinner, everyone at the table kept checking their mobile devices (choosing budgeted presence). She said, "I couldn't believe it. There were about fifteen relatives sitting around the table and they had not seen each other in months. The television was on in the background and no one was really talking except to comment on the food. My family would have never allowed phones at the table at Thanksgiving. It felt really awkward." One chief financial officer from one banking organization told me that his CEO forbid use of mobile devices in meetings: "If he sees your phone out during a meeting, you have to leave the meeting since you are obviously not invested in the conversation. It only took a few of those times before no one brought their phone to meetings."

How Soon Do You Need to Respond?

How quickly you need to respond to the message also relates to context. One of the challenges of carrying a mobile device with you all the time is that you are *technically available* all the time. Only you can make the choice of whether you are actually available. So, if you know you are going to be in a situation that might require invitational presence, you need to make sure you have not given someone else the expectation that you are available. When I was talking with college students about times when they had a successful interaction with their parents about a serious topic, most of them discussed the importance they placed on their parents silencing their mobile devices. One student said, "I actually have a hard time coming up with a good example of a conversation because my Dad is always on his phone. He is either playing a game or checking his email or messages. When I try to talk to him, he says he is listening, but I see he isn't. So, I just don't talk to him anymore. He is just background noise to me in the house."

Can Anyone See You?

Visibility is an important element of context because you may be hurting someone's feelings or making them think you are not focusing on their message if you are texting someone else at the same time. If you choose budgeted presence and your audience can see you, you are signaling that their conversation does not require your full attention. During COVID-19, when many people found themselves on videoconferencing calls throughout the day, the term "Zoom exhaustion" emerged. People found themselves worn out from focusing so hard on their video screens throughout the day. One of the managers of a nonprofit told me that

> an audioconference is easy. I can be in the conversation while I am doing my laundry and text my colleagues. I can easily do a task like that in the middle of the conversation. But a videoconference is exhausting. I have to focus so hard on looking into the camera to make sure I look interested, so no one is distracted by my face. I have to act so much more interested on video than I would even have to do face-to-face. Those meetings just aren't that interesting. It is just day after day of pretense.

Do You Have Time?

Time is also an important element to consider when thinking about your context. If you don't have very much time for a conversation, it is difficult to choose invitational presence. If you are pressed for time to respond to many different audiences, you might need to choose budgeted presence. However, when making this choice, explicitly discussing the time constraints and the reason that you are not focusing only on your audience's conversation might help you to convince the audience that your choice makes sense. If you are in charge of a meeting and you need people to focus for a specific period to hear what you have to say, it might make sense to choose entitled. But remember, entitled is efficient only when it works and everyone listens. A shortage of time also may be the prompt for invitational rather than budgeted social presence. Members of a work team may decide collectively that, because they have very little time for solving a problem, they need everyone's perspective and invite everyone to set their mobile devices aside and focus on the problem at hand, thus deciding to choose invitational social presence.

How Big Is Your Audience?

The size of your audience can directly connect to accountability, engagement, and influence. The larger your audience, the less control you have over their use of their technology. You can actually make the same argument with size of audience and response expectations, which essentially leads to engagement. You have probably noticed this most dramatically in videoconferencing conversations. The larger the number of people on the call, the harder it is for interaction to happen. In a large face-to-face audience, you also face this interaction problem, but at least you are sharing the same physical space and can rely on the audience to do policing of each other. Over video, the larger the audience becomes, the harder it is to view any one individual, which gives your audience a feeling of anonymity. During COVID-19, businesses and schools quickly realized the impossibility of choosing entitled presence since the meeting itself required their audience's devices to be on. Larger audiences also can create challenges for invitational presence because of the decrease in interactivity and necessarily the difficulty of creating a partnership with your audience.

WHAT IS YOUR MESSAGE?

Your message helps to determine your choice of presence. The charac-teristics of sensitivity, salience, complexity, and ambiguity, as well as the goal of your message, are helpful to consider. If your message is sensitive, you might consider choices that are more audience focused. Sensitive messages require an attention to your audiences and an understanding of how they might be receiving that message. A performance review with an employee giving them critical feedback about negative performance, a conversation with a friend about a challenge they are facing, or telling someone you are ending a relationship are all conversations that might require a sensitivity to the audience and therefore your careful consider-ation of your choice of presence. Even messages that are more celebratory require a sensitivity to the emotion of the moment. When someone gives you great news and you don't respond with the appropriate emotion, you are not focusing on the needs of your audience. Most people with whom I have talked about presence have shared a story about feeling hurt, disre-spected, or ignored by communicators who were on their digital devices.

Saliency of messages is also helpful to consider. Messages that are critical require an attention to the message. When you are on your mobile device and are distracted while communicating a message, it is very hard to simultaneously communicate that you think that message matters. If you think your message is important, you need to make sure your audi-ence thinks the message is important too. Choosing entitled presence because you think the message is critical can work only if the audience also thinks the message is critical. If you choose entitled presence and your audience does not, you will lose your credibility as a speaker.

Complicated or confusing messages require focus. Choosing bud-geted presence necessarily means you are multitasking. You can do this with a simple message but not with a complicated or complex message that requires attention and concentration. Conversations involving topics that are not very complicated probably don't need the focus of more seri-ous or salient conversations, so budgeted presence might make sense for those interactions. A very serious conversation might demand entitled presence because you need the focus from your audience. More ambiguous conversations—involving topics like "What is the best future strategy?" or "What career should I consider?"—might require more input and involvement from your audience. Ambiguous conversations don't have a clear answer. They might require more dialogue. I will talk about these more as I discuss your relationship with your audience.

Finally, your goal is critically important to your presence choice. Budgeted and entitled presence choices are more about your efficiency, while competitive and invitational focus more on your audience and their needs. If your goal is efficiency, you might choose budgeted or entitled. If your goal is to persuade, you would lean more toward choosing competitive presence. Finally, if your primary goal is sharing information and learning, you might choose invitational presence.

WHO IS YOUR AUDIENCE?

Your audience is another important element to consider when choosing presence. Critical elements include how much you value your audience, your status in relationship with your audience, and how interdependent you are with your audience. Your attention signals how much you value a conversation or person. When someone hears you typing on your keyboard or sees you in budgeted presence, you are signaling to that person that the conversation is not worth your full attention at that time. Budgeted and entitled presence are much more about you getting your own tasks accomplished than about your audience. Competitive and invitational presence are more focused on the needs of your audience. Competitive presence recognizes the need to frame your message in terms of your audience's primary interests. Invitational presence is fully focused on your audience, in that you see your audience as a partner. You signal the value you give your audience to the extent that you include them in your choice of presence. Some people I have talked with think entitled presence is also about your audience. For example, some faculty members have told me, "I take my student's mobile devices away from them in my class for their own good. They will thank me later." However, your choice of entitled presence suggests that you can't trust your audience to make "the right choice and listen to you," so it also signals that you don't value their ability to make the "right" decision.

Your status is also important. The more power you have in a relationship, the easier it is to choose entitled presence. Whether your status comes from your position within the organization or the family, the more authority you have in a specific context, the more likely your audience will be to acquiesce to your demands concerning their mobile devices. Many of the high school students I surveyed, when asked when they might turn off their phones, listed during dinner, because "my parents have a rule about no cell phones at the table." As a leader in your organization, you also have the ability to set norms and rules for how your employees will use their mobile devices. However, it is important to make sure that you don't have competing expectations where you expect quick responses to organizational messages and you also expect employees to silence their devices during meetings.

Finally, interdependence is an important relationship issue to consider. Even if you don't value the relationship, if you are interdependent with your audience and you need them to accomplish a task or you need their support for an initiative, you need to signal to them that they matter. Continuously choosing budgeted presence during a conversation creates limitations in how focused you can be on that specific conversation. You might miss nonverbal cues or important words that could help you better understand your audience. Similarly, choosing entitled or competitive presence focuses the message on your needs but might not foster a feeling of openness in your audience, and both you and your audience will be less inclined to engage in a dialogue and learn from each other. Choosing invitational presence means you will not be able to get as much content across as with the other presence choices, but you may put yourself in a better mind-set for you to learn from your audience. The more interdependent you are with your audience, the more you may need to accept this trade-off.

WHAT HAPPENS WHEN YOU AND YOUR AUDIENCE
DON'T AGREE?

While I have been focusing the conversation on your choice of presence for a specific situation, keep in mind that you can't control your audience. Many times, you might choose one type of presence to fit your own needs but find that your audience has chosen something different. Communication requires that both sides come to an agreement on the way a conversation will be approached. Consider that each conversation on which you embark is created by everyone involved, not just you. I like to think of conversations as co-created by all the participants. Your success in choosing a specific type of presence is contingent on your audience supporting you or at least allowing you to make that choice.

Mismatches between your choice of presence and what your audience expects to be able to choose usually result in dissatisfaction—ranging from mild frustration to anger, or from concern to disappointment. Common examples of mismatches include times when a communicator chooses entitled and the audience chooses budgeted. For example, a university professor asks students to put their mobile devices away and she still sees people in her class using their mobile devices. Or another example could be when the communicator chooses budgeted presence and the audience expects invitational presence. A manager might be conducting a performance review while at the same time texting a colleague about a sales figure. The employee receiving the performance review was hoping for a dialogue and feels like the manager doesn't even care.

Each of the factors that I discussed above that drive your choice of a specific type of presence also drive your audience's perception of their own presence choice. When you and your audience agree on the perception of those factors, the likelihood for a match is higher. For example, when both you and your audience believe a conversation is sensitive and critical and requires a dialogue where both communicators can learn from each other, the choice of invitational presence can be productive.

In contrast, when communicators have different perceptions of these factors, a mismatch can occur. For example, during the COVID-19 pandemic, when people needed to bring their work into their homes during quarantine, many families felt the stress of negotiating different perceptions regarding presence. One person told me about the misunderstanding her children had about her work and conference calls:

> I will be in the middle of a videoconference and my teenager will come into the room upset about something someone posted in social media. She thinks I am available to talk because she sees me sitting there on a call on mute. But if I move my head and start talking to her, everyone on the call will see me! She thinks I don't care about her anymore because she always sees me in my office working. It used to be I could turn off work when I came into the house but now work is in my house all the time. I feel like she is always upset with me.

With the juggling of work and home that people experienced during the pandemic, I have heard many examples just like these of mismatches between what one communicator expects in the choice of presence and what the other communicator chooses. The physical location no longer contains the conversation, and therefore there are more options available to both communicators. Students are in class but also in their bedroom or are connecting from a car or a parking lot with better Wi-Fi. An executive is in a meeting but also in his kitchen. A doctor is in a visit with a patient while also in her home office. A manager is talking with a team member while also managing her third-grader's attention to a virtual classroom activity. These infrastructure changes have placed additional stress on conversations that have exacerbated the difficulties associated with the ubiquitous mobile device.

Here is another example of a mismatch within the area of telemedicine. I actually wrote my dissertation on the use of telemedicine as a means of medical delivery within the prison system, so I have been studying telemedicine for over twenty-five years. With the pandemic's lockdown preventing many people from seeing a doctor in person, more specialties have turned to telemedicine as a means to connect with their patients and telemedicine use has skyrocketed.[1] This dramatic change in delivery for some patients and providers has had an impact on the dialogue that might normally be perceived as invitational. I saw this in an example that a therapist shared with me about her telepsychology practice. In her practice, she sees children of all ages. Since the pandemic, she has had people talk to her while in the McDonald's drive-through lane, shopping at Walmart, in the waiting room of a dentist's office, in the emergency room, and making dinner for the family. Each of her patients signs paperwork committing to the importance of a secure telecommunication connection and environment and the need to be focused during the session. However, the freedom to participate in other activities while also taking care of their therapy seems hard to resist. One of her thirteen-year-old patients was interrupted by her mother during the session to come downstairs and get in the car to go pick up a sibling. Said the therapist, "I was on the video call being carried through the house on the phone and then I was riding in the car with the patient's mother. Then the mother started asking me questions about the visit while she was driving. When I suggested that we probably shouldn't have the conversation while she was driving, the mother said, 'Don't worry, I am not holding the phone while I am driving!'"

This situation describes a clear mismatch of presence choices. The therapist is choosing invitational presence and the patient and the patient's mother are choosing budgeted presence. This mismatch is based on a fundamental misunderstanding of expectations regarding a therapy conversation. The patient and mother never had the option to walk or drive around during a therapy appointment, so the need for clarifying these expectations never came up until the pandemic. An example of a mismatch of expectations that received considerable media attention was a California plastic surgeon who arrived for his virtual traffic violation court appearance from the operating room. He appeared on video with his surgical team in the background as they were operating on a patient. Though not technically budgeted presence—because the surgeon insisted that he was going to focus on the virtual court meeting while he let his colleagues continue the operation—the background activity of the operating room was distracting and unexpected.[2] The COVID pandemic provided flexibility surrounding the communicator's choice of location and timing, creating additional challenges for negotiating mediated conversations.

HOW CAN YOU NEGOTIATE YOUR PRESENCE CHOICE WITHIN YOUR CONVERSATIONS?

In my conversations with people about their use of mobile devices, I have been struck by the *lack* of conversation about mobile device use. While mobile devices tend to be a part of or can intrude into every interaction, communicators seem reluctant to address or acknowledge that they can and should address this challenge.

Entitled presence is the only presence choice where you explicitly tell someone to put their device away. But each type of presence could involve a conversation about your expectations regarding mobile device use or your ideas about the need to focus on one conversation. However, even with entitled presence, communicators don't often explicitly address the mismatch. For example, one manager told me that she started her meetings telling people to silence their mobile devices. Then she told me about one guy who never paid attention to her opening directive: "He would just sit there and continue to text. It was like he didn't care. He drives me crazy." When I asked the manager if she ever said anything to him about it, she responded, "He knows what he is doing. I don't need to tell him." However, while she told everyone to silence their devices, by not talking to him directly when he continued to text, she implied that his behavior was acceptable.

As I have talked with people about both their use of mobile devices in the home and workplace, they often talk about being frustrated or angry with a mismatch of expectations regarding mobile device use. However, while they are frustrated, they don't see a reason to explicitly talk about it. Most of the time, the person said that they "didn't want to be rude" or that they "didn't want to seem old-fashioned." So they remained silent but upset. However, the ubiquitous nature of mobile devices means that you need to figure out a way to communicate with your audiences about your expectations for mobile device use. It is often unlikely that you and your audience will see the use of mobile devices in the same way, so setting up your expectations or starting a conversation with your audience about the use of devices or the focus of the conversation is important.

THREE CHOICES AVAILABLE TO YOU WHEN FACING MISMATCHES

You basically have three possible choices when facing a mismatch: *give in to your communicator's choice, ignore or overlook their choice,* or *actively discuss the mismatch.* Let's discuss each of these options so you can make a more informed decision about the implications of your choice.

Your first option when faced with a mismatch with your audience is to give in to their choice—to acquiesce. What do I mean? Giving in to another communicator's choice of presence means that you are allowing that person or group of people to dictate your choice of presence. For example, your boss asks you to put your mobile device away while she is speaking, and you acquiesce or give in, even though you know it is not the most efficient use of your time. In another situation, you might have your audience give in to you. For example, you decide that you don't believe your family should have mobile devices at the dinner table, so you tell everyone to put their devices away. However, each person explains how he or she is waiting for an important call or is supposed to be available for work. So you give in. You convince yourself that you don't care about people being on their devices at the dinner table and that maybe they have a point. And you change your rule.

There are many reasons why you might decide to give in to someone else's choice of presence. You might decide that you will give in to your audience's choice of presence to get something else that you want. One woman I talked with said that her husband always played a game on his phone while they were talking. She said it used to drive her crazy. But she realized, "He just can't sit still. He says playing a game on his device while we talk helps him to concentrate. I don't know if I believe it or not, but it is not worth the fight. So, we usually just spend the evening playing games on our phones and talking every once in a while. We never get into a deep conversation."

Many other people I talked with would give in because, in their words, "It just isn't worth the fight. I can't make someone pay attention to me." Status could be another reason to acquiesce. If your boss tells you to put your technology away and listen to his presentation, you are probably not going to get into an argument with him about his choice. You will just put your mobile device away.

When you choose to give in to your audience's choice of presence, the conversation or situation takes place with one presence type—specifically, the one your audience chose. You let go of your own perspective regarding presence and adopt the approach of your audience. Giving in can be effective if you convince yourself that you are OK with this decision. However, if you give in and then become bitter and resentful because you let the other person have their way, you may take this frustration out on the relationship. When you don't explicitly say that you are giving in, but you just give in to yourself but stay mad, you are missing out on a chance to address the mismatch explicitly. If I don't know that you are mad about my choice of presence, how can I find a way to come to an understanding?

Another way to negotiate presence choices when you're facing a mismatch is to overlook the behavior. Overlooking the behavior is different from giving in. When you overlook someone else's behavior, you still keep your own choice of presence and the other person keeps their choice of presence. Instead of giving in, you choose to ignore their choice. A common example of overlooking can be seen in a classroom or meeting when the presenter tells everyone to put their mobile devices away and some students just keep texting or checking their mobile devices. The presenter still chooses entitled presence and wants her audience to put their technology away. She sees that they haven't, but she doesn't call the offenders out on their behavior. Here, the presenter is just overlooking the audience's behavior. Many people believe their mobile device use is invisible to others, but it is usually apparent in either the focus of their eyes or their delay in responding immediately during a conversation. Students often think that their professor does not see them texting in the back row of the classroom. In fact, the professor often does see that members of the class have chosen budgeted presence even though she wrote on the syllabus to not bring mobile devices to class. But instead of calling out the behavior, the professor just overlooks it.

A challenge to consider with overlooking someone's choice and continuing with your own is that your audience might think that you don't really care. Let's return to the presentation example. If you tell people to put their devices away and some people keep texting during your presentation, and you still don't say anything about their behavior, you are communicating that it doesn't matter to you. Other people in the class or seminar who are following your choice of entitled presence see the behavior of others and may decide that you don't really care about whether they are on their phone. At a minimum, you are confusing your audience because what you said you wanted and the behavior you are accepting don't match. Now people don't know whether to follow your choice. Remember, I said some people give in or acquiesce because you have status over them or because they want a favor from you later. When you overlook your audience's behavior, you are sending the signal that their sacrifice to give in to your choice of presence does not matter to you.

When you choose to overlook your audience's choice of presence, the conversation or interaction takes place with two types of presence in place. You may continue to choose entitled presence while your audience is choosing budgeted. Unlike with the first option of giving in, you continue to try to engage your audience in entitled presence, but you don't say anything to address those individuals who are ignoring you.

A final choice for you to consider when facing a mismatch is actively discussing the mismatch with your audience or partner. This final choice involves an explicit conversation that each member of the interaction has about the use of mobile devices, so that your ideas and theirs are shared. You and your fellow communicators are "co-creating" the communication environment together, so expectations and assumptions are clear and set. This choice involves communicating about your communication, or "metacommunicating." For example, a CEO before a board meeting has a conversation about the use of digital devices. She suggests that people should focus on the board meeting and would like people to put their mobile devices away and only focus on the meeting. Then she asks for input from her audience. Some of the board members at the meeting might say they have a couple of colleagues to whom they will need to respond throughout the meeting but that they will only use their devices for those specific conversations and will try not to distract when they address those calls. In this case, the group has negotiated to stay mainly in entitled presence except for the few calls that will require budgeted presence.

You also might have a conversation about splitting up a meeting. You might discuss the possibility of starting a meeting in competitive presence, where participants could access devices, but then ask for the focus of invitational presence and dialogue during the last half of the meeting. The primary point here is to recognize that when you choose a type of social presence with another communicator to have a conversation, your choice about how you will have the conversation can be just as important as the conversation itself.

Mobile devices are a critical part of your everyday life. Research has shown you should acknowledge these devices and advocate your perspective regarding them. For example, if you choose entitled presence, you might explain why. You could say to your team, "We have a number of difficult issues to talk about today and I think it would be helpful if we all focused on this conversation and silenced our devices. I will keep this meeting to no more than 45 minutes. What are your thoughts about that approach?" This statement helps to explain the rationale behind your choice of entitled presence and asks for their buy-in.

Just because you have a conversation about how you will communicate doesn't mean that you will always get your way. For example, your boss tells you to put your mobile devices away during a meeting and you explain your concern—that you are waiting for a message from an important client, so you say you will focus on your boss's conversation but need to monitor your device for that other message. If your boss still doesn't agree, and tells you to ignore all calls, at least you have had your priorities established. She understands your goals for the meeting and she also doesn't see you looking at your phone and make assumptions that you are not serious about your work.

After your conversation with your conversational partner about your disagreement with their choice of presence, you might then move to the options of giving in or overlooking if you and your audience don't agree. Or you might decide to walk away from the conversation. But at least you have explicitly talked about your preferences for the conversation and the risk of misunderstanding is reduced.

HOW CAN YOU COMMUNICATE THESE STRATEGIES?

Because communicating about something you have never had to communicate about before—namely, telling another person how you want to be present—is difficult, we avoid the conversation. To help give you some ideas about how to have these conversations, here are some ideas under each category of presence:

Budgeted:
- (When you need to be in budgeted): I know this conversation is important, but I have another (meeting, message, update, etc.) that I am expecting from (my family, an important client, a close friend). As a result, I need to be on my mobile device during your (presentation, conversation, board meeting). I will try to stay as focused on your message as I can because I know it is important.
- (When facing budgeted in a conversation): I notice you seem to need to check your phone a lot. Are you really busy right now, or do you have time to talk? If you don't I understand, we can reschedule for another time.
- (When facing someone who is usually in budgeted and is interrupting your other choices): Over the weekend, I received a number of emails from you, and I want to make sure I understand your expectations for these emails. How soon would you like to see a response after I receive your email or text, and is there a way we can work out an arrangement so that I can be respon-

sive to you during the weekend? (This conversation allows you to set expectations and assumptions—some people send a text when they are thinking about it but not when they need you to respond.)

Entitled:

- For the next 10 minutes, I would like you to focus on this one conversation so that you can better understand _____, which will help you to achieve _____. I know you may have other commitments right now, but I promise to be brief.
- I have created an agenda for the meeting and have included several breaks for you to check your phone or take care of any tasks that come up. We will not be going more than 30 minutes without a break. Will that give you enough time to take care of your messages so we can focus on the meeting?
- Can we both agree to put our phones away during this conversation?
- I have a great idea to consider for our new campaign. Can I have your full attention for the next 10 minutes so I can go over it with you?

For the competitive presence choice, the script is not as necessary because your goal is to use influence and audience-centered communication in such a compelling way that your audience doesn't want to engage in any conversation but yours. However, people have shared with me many strategies they use to get the attention of the audience. Some people make a joke about the fact that their audience is on their phones. During COVID-19, when I was teaching, I would often bring up the challenge students faced in attending class virtually while they were on the same device that served as their distraction from my message. I hoped that by bringing up the awareness of the problem, it might help my audience recognize that presence is a choice made on a moment-by-moment basis, so they need to be intentional about that choice. A number of people shared the strategy of silence as a nonverbal but communicative way to get the attention of the audience. One person said, "When I am talking and my friend is on her phone, I just stop talking. I wait for her to notice and then I go back to my story."

Competitive:
- If you need to check in with your email right now, I understand. I will check back when you are done.
- I see you are really busy right now but I would love to connect. If you need to take care of that, we can talk later.

Invitational:
- We are facing a (complex, critical, sensitive) challenge, and we need to work together to (solve, address, learn from) this situation. Do you have some time to talk about this?
- I am happy we are having dinner because something happened that I need to talk with you about and I would love to get your thoughts on this. Would you be open to have this conversation now?
- Invitational presence might even require being explicit about your goal: I haven't had the chance to talk with you for a while, and I would really like to hear how you are doing. Do you have time to catch up with me?

Invitational presence might require a prompt to get you started. For example, you can find questions that can stimulate conversations online. The psychologist Arthur Aron wrote a famous set of questions that were widely published, including in the *New York Times*, "The 36 Questions That Lead to Love."[3]

These questions lead to more self-disclosure and create connections through mutual vulnerability. They include questions like "What would constitute a "perfect" day for you?" or "What is your most treasured memory?" and end with deeper questions like "If you were to die this evening with no opportunity to communicate with anyone, what would you most regret not having told someone? Why haven't you told them yet?"

These scripts are just ideas to get you started. You obviously need to create a conversation starter that works for you. The main thing to remember is to address the potential for your conversation to be interrupted before you even start.

BE INTENTIONAL ABOUT YOUR PRESENCE CHOICE IN EVERY CONVERSATION

Choosing presence is not something that happens once in a conversation but a choice that happens on a moment-by-moment basis. It is not a choice about turning your phone off or keeping it on. It is a choice that involves examining your context, your audience, and your message. Your mobile device has brought you great efficiencies and opportunities for communication. You can participate in more conversations now than ever before. With this power comes a responsibility to choose intentionally and wisely. The success of every conversation depends on it.

NOTES

1. Andrei Zimiles, "Four New Statistics That Prove That Telemedicine Isn't Just a Pandemic Fad," *Medical Economics*, www.medicaleconomics.com/view/four-new -statistics-that-prove-that-telemedicine-isn-t-just-a-pandemic-fad.

2. Marie Fazio, "Plastic Surgeon Attends Video Traffic Court from Operating Room," February 28, 2021, www.nytimes.com/2021/02/28/us/california-surgeon -zoom-traffic-violation-court.html.

3. Mandy Len Catron, "To Fall in Love with Anyone, Do This," *New York Times*, January 9, 2015, www.nytimes.com/2015/01/11/style/modern-love-to-fall-in-love -with-anyone-do-this.html.

Suggested Reading

Bauerlein, Mark, ed. *The Digital Divide: Arguments for and against Facebook, Google, Texting, and the Age of Social Networking.* New York: Jeremy P. Tarcher / Penguin, 2011.

boyd, danah. *It's Complicated: The Social Lives of Networked Teens.* New Haven, CT: Yale University Press, 2014.

Burgoon, Judee K., Laura K. Guerrero, and Valerie Manusov. *Nonverbal Communication.* New York: Routledge, 2016.

Cialdini, Robert B. *Influence: The Psychology of Persuasion.* New York: HarperCollins, 1993.

Cohen, Allan R., and David L. Bradford. *Influence without Authority.* Hoboken, NJ: John Wiley & Sons, 2017.

Crenshaw, Dave. *The Myth of Multitasking: How "Doing It All" Gets Nothing Done.* San Francisco: Jossey-Bass, 2008.

Cuddy, Amy. *Presence: Bringing Your Boldest Self to Your Biggest Challenges.* New York: Little, Brown, 2015.

Davenport, Thomas H., and John C. Beck. *The Attention Economy: Understanding the New Currency of Business.* Boston: Harvard Business Review Press, 2001.

Duarte, Nancy. *Resonate: Present Visual Stories That Transform Audiences.* Hoboken, NJ: John Wiley & Sons, 2013.

———. *Slide:ology: The Art and Science of Creating Great Presentations.* Sebastopol, CA: O'Reilly Media, 2008.

Edmondson, Amy C. The *Fearless Organization: Creating Psychological Safety in the Workplace for Learning, Innovation, and Growth.* Hoboken, NJ: John Wiley & Sons, 2018.

Foss, Karen A., and Robert Trapp. *Contemporary Perspectives on Rhetoric.* Long Grove, IL: Waveland Press, 2014.

Foss, Sonja K., and Karen A. Foss. *Inviting Transformation: Presentational Speaking for a Changing World, Fourth Edition.* Long Grove, IL: Waveland Press, 2019.

Gladwell, Malcolm. *Talking to Strangers: What We Should Know about the People We Don't Know.* New York: Little, Brown, 2019.

Grant, Adam M. *Give and Take: A Revolutionary Approach to Success*. London: Weidenfeld & Nicolson, 2014.

Heath, Chip, and Dan Heath. *Decisive: How to Make Better Choices in Life and Work*. Toronto: Random House of Canada, 2013.

———. *Made to Stick: Why Some Ideas Survive and Others Die*. New York: Random House, 2007.

———. *Switch: How to Change Things When Change Is Hard*. New York: Crown, 2010.

Heifetz, Ronald A., Marty Linsky, and Alexander Grashow. *The Practice of Adaptive Leadership: Tools and Tactics for Changing Your Organization and the World*. Boston: Harvard Business Review Press, 2009.

Jenkins, Henry, Mizuko Ito, and danah boyd. *Participatory Culture in a Networked Era: A Conversation on Youth, Learning, Commerce, and Politics*. Hoboken, NJ: John Wiley & Sons, 2015.

Kelley, Harold H., and John W. Thibaut. *Interpersonal Relations: A Theory of Interdependence*. Hoboken, NJ: Wiley, 1978.

Martin, James. *The Jesuit Guide to (Almost) Everything: A Spirituality for Real Life*. New York: HarperCollins, 2010.

Meyrowitz, Joshua. *No Sense of Place: The Impact of Electronic Media on Social Behavior*. New York: Oxford University Press, 1985.

Morgan, Nick. *Can You Hear Me? How to Connect with People in a Virtual World*. Boston: Harvard Business Review Press, 2018.

———. *Power Cues: The Subtle Science of Leading Groups, Persuading Others, and Maximizing Your Personal Impact*. Boston: Harvard Business Review Press, 2014.

———. *Trust Me: Four Steps to Authenticity and Charisma*. Hoboken, NJ: John Wiley & Sons, 2008.

Munter, Mary, and Lynn Hamilton. *Guide to Managerial Communication*. 10th edition. Boston: Pearson, 2013.

Murphy, Kate. *You're Not Listening: What You're Missing and Why It Matters*. New York: Celadon Books, 2020.

Newport, Cal. *Digital Minimalism: Choosing a Focused Life in a Noisy World*. New York: Penguin, 2019.

Parr, Ben. *Captivology: The Science of Capturing People's Attention*. New York: HarperCollins, 2015.

Patterson, Kerry, Joseph Grenny, Ron McMillan, and Al Switzler. *Crucial Conversations Tools for Talking When Stakes Are High, Second Edition*. New York: McGraw Hill Professional, 2011.

Perlow, Leslie A. *Sleeping with Your Smartphone: How to Break the 24/7 Habit and Change the Way You Work*. Boston: Harvard Business Review Press, 2012.

Puhl, Louis J., trans. and ed. *The Spiritual Exercises of St. Ignatius: A New Translation Based on Studies in the Language of the Autograph*. Chicago: Loyola Press, 1951.

Rainie, Harrison, Lee Rainie, and Barry Wellman. Networked: *The New Social Operating System*. Cambridge, MA: MIT Press, 2014.

Senge, Peter, and C. Scharmer. *Presence: Exploring Profound Change in People, Organizations, and Society*. Boston: Nicholas Brealey, 2011.

Shapira, Allison. *Speak with Impact: How to Command the Room and Influence Others*. New York: AMACOM, 2018.

Short, John, Ederyn Williams, and Bruce Christie. *The Social Psychology of Telecommunications*. Hoboken, NJ: John Wiley & Sons, 1976.

Stephens, Keri K. *Negotiating Control: Organizations and Mobile Communication*. New York: Oxford University Press, 2018.

Stone, Douglas F., Douglas Stone, Bruce Patton, and Sheila Heen. *Difficult Conversations: How to Discuss What Matters Most*. New York: Penguin Books, 2000.

Stone, Douglas, and Sheila Heen. *Thanks for the Feedback: The Science and Art of Receiving Feedback Well (Even When It Is Off Base, Unfair, Poorly Delivered, and Frankly, You're Not in the Mood)*. New York: Penguin, 2015.

Turkle, Sherry. *Alone Together: Why We Expect More from Technology and Less from Each Other*. New York: Basic Books, 2012.

———. *Life on the Screen*. New York: Simon & Schuster, 2011.

———. *Reclaiming Conversation: The Power of Talk in a Digital Age*. New York: Penguin Press, 2015.

Index

asynchronicity, 36–37
always on, 16
audience: budgeted presence and,
    32–33; choice of presence and,
    164–65, 168, 170–75; competitive
    presence and, 99–106, 110, 125–26;
    as container, 75–76; disagreement
    with, 172–75; disrespecting, 38–39,
    86; entitled presence and, 75–76,
    79, 81; evidence and, 102–3; freedom
    of, 140–41; groupings structure
    and, 102; invitational presence and,
    142–43, 145–46, 162; safety felt by,
    140; social capital and, 72; valuing
    of, 140
autism, 52
availability, continuous, as norm,
    29–30

Bies, Bob, 41
body language, 103–4
breakout rooms, 159
broadcasting, interaction *vs.*, 53
Brown, Jason, 77
budgeted presence: audience and,
    32–33; benefits of, 35–37; classroom
    and, 57–61; communication of,
    180–81; defined, 14–15, 26–30; family
    and, 53–57; focus of control in, 33–35;
    friendships and, 51–53; invitational
    presence and, 133, 149–50, 161–62;
    messages and, 169–70; outside
    workplace, 48–64; relationship
    factors and, 63; students and, 59–61;
    technological triage and, 30–32;
    trade-offs with, 37–40; when to

choose, 40–44, 61–64; in workplace,
    25–46

capital, social, 72, 78
children, 48–49. *See also* classroom;
    family
choice of presence: audience and, 164–
    65, 168, 170–75; context in, 165–68;
    giving in to that of another, 176–77;
    interdependence and, 171; message
    in, 165, 169–70; negotiating, within
    conversation, 175–76; norms and,
    166; status and, 171; time and,
    167–68; visibility and, 167
classroom, 57–61, 90–93; competitive
    presence and, 120–24; flipped, 123;
    invitational presence and, 156–60
cognitive complexity, 56
collaborative environment, 140–42
commitment strategy, 117
competitive presence, 15; audience and,
    99–103, 110, 125–26; body language
    and, 103–4; clarity and, 101; in
    classroom, 120–24; communication
    of, 182; defined, 99–100; faculty and,
    121–23; family and, 118–20; focus of
    control in, 106–7; friendships and,
    115–18; goal of, 114; key elements
    of, 100–104; main theme and, 101,
    112; norms and, 114–15; outside
    workplace, 114–26; relevance and,
    107–8; students and, 92–93; trade-
    offs in, 107–8; when to use, 108–10,
    124–26; in workplace, 99–110
compliance-gaining strategies, 116
conclusions, 113

About the Author

Jeanine W. Turner is a professor at Georgetown University in the Communication, Culture, and Technology Program and is an affiliated faculty member of the McDonough School of Business. She inspires and challenges executives to gain a strengthened sense of how best to communicate their presence in a variety of environments. Her research and coursework explore persuasion, conflict resolution, and the impact of new media on organizational and interpersonal communication. When leading executive programs, she provides concrete skills and strategies for delivering information and messages as well as specific tools for managing difficult conversations. She received a PhD in communications from the Ohio State University.